Working with Words

CAREERS FOR WRITERS

Working with Words
CAREERS FOR WRITERS

Margaret Harmon, Editor

THE WESTMINSTER PRESS
Philadelphia

Book Design by Dorothy Alden Smith

PUBLISHED BY THE WESTMINSTER PRESS®
PHILADELPHIA, PENNSYLVANIA

PRINTED IN THE UNITED STATES OF AMERICA

Library of Congress Cataloging in Publication Data

Main entry under title:

Working with words.

   Bibliography: p.
   Includes index.
   SUMMARY: Discusses employment opportunities and educational preparation for writing jobs ranging from technical editing and proofreading to writing news copy.
   1. Authorship. [1. Authorship. 2. Vocational guidance] I. Harmon, Margaret.
PN153.W6   808'.0023   76–57192
ISBN 0–664–32610–2

Contents

Contributors 7

1. WRITERS AND OTHER COMMUNICATORS *9*

2. NEWS MEDIA
   Robert Roth *13*

3. MAGAZINES
   John A. McNichol, Jr. *30*

4. ADVERTISING
   Robert Ensinger *36*

5. TECHNICAL WRITING
   Joseph Chapline *49*

6. RADIO AND TELEVISION
   Margaret Harmon *70*

7. BOOK PUBLISHING
   Margaret Harmon *79*

8. EDUCATION: PROGRAMS AND COURSES *111*

Bibliography *143*

Index *147*

Contributors

The contributors to this book are all experienced in their respective fields. Robert Roth dropped out of college and got his first newspaper job (he can't recall ever wanting any other kind of job) through the shameless exercise of pull. It was on the Newark *Star Eagle* at $17.50 a week, and he worked mostly on police assignments—which included coverage of a Ku Klux Klan murder. Then he moved to the *Yonkers Herald,* where his beat was city politics, and political observation has been his line ever since. He has been actively engaged in coverage of every major party convention since 1944. He advanced to city editor on the *Yonkers Herald* and then to managing editor on the *Mt. Vernon Argus.* He then moved to the big time on the *Philadelphia Record* and after two years became Washington bureau chief. The *Record* was sold, and after a brief stint on the *Daily News* in New York he joined the Philadelphia *Bulletin.* From 1954 to 1968 he was chief of the *Bulletin*'s Washington bureau, and since then has been a columnist for that paper.

John A. McNichol, Jr., was educated at LaSalle College and Columbia University. Formerly New Directions editor of the Chilton Company's *EE/Systems*

Engineering Today, he is now a management consultant.

Robert Ensinger has a B.S. in communications from Temple University. He has been director of advertising and public relations for Philco-Ford, CRC Chemicals, and other companies, and is now an account executive with Ted Thomas Associates, Inc., an advertising agency. He has also been chief announcer for an FM station—a natural job, since he studied voice and opera at the Curtis Institute of Music. He now uses his musical talents in conducting the Robert Ensinger Chorale.

Joseph Chapline, a graduate of Ursinus College, worked with Eckert and Mauchly on the early BINAC and UNIVAC electronic computers, preparing all their engineering reports and manuals of instruction for publication. He later directed report-writing groups for the Philco Corporation and now writes technical documents and also teaches writing courses for employees of various industries. Chapline is also a professional musician and has built and rebuilt pipe organs for a number of clients.

Margaret Harmon, a graduate of Bryn Mawr College, has worked as a copy editor for magazines and for a publishing house and has been a technical writer in industry. She has published two books on semitechnical subjects.

1

Writers and Other Communicators

When we think of a writer, our minds may conjure up a picture of a genius in an attic spinning great poems and stories the way a silkworm spins a cocoon. The writer does this by a kind of compulsion or inspiration, whether or not anybody buys or even reads the works produced.

There have been and still are such geniuses. Some, like John Keats and Emily Dickinson, spin such silken threads. Others, like Shakespeare, weave the woof of ordinary life upon a warp of insight. Shakespeare, however, had an eye to the public taste, since he was a member of a commercial dramatic company. And so do many present writers who, if they work in attics, do so in the hope of earning enough money for better accommodations, where they can continue to turn out articles and books, and try to sell them to magazines and book publishers. These are the free-lance writers.

There is another class of writers who don't work in ivory towers or even on the kitchen table. They go to work in the morning, put in their eight hours like everybody else, and fight their way home in the traffic at night. These are the staff writers—on the staff of an employer who pays them wages and expects them to produce a certain amount of writing every day to order. The great majority of writers today belong to this class. Some of them may write up information supplied by others. Technical writers put together the ideas and information of engineers and other scientists. Newswriters put together stories from facts supplied by reporters and researchers. Other newsmen and newswomen go out and get their own material, and so do some staff writers for magazines. But even though their work is more or less under the control of management, staff writers must have a good knowledge of the subjects they write about. The reporter is no longer a former copyboy who has worked his way up. He has probably studied economics and politics in college, just as the science writer has studied some science and the sportswriter knows sports—perhaps from experience as a player or a coach. The advertising writer knows the product and the market.

Many free-lance writers are former staff writers who have gone into business for themselves. Hemingway and other famous writers started as reporters. And many free-lance writers have been offered good staff jobs on magazines after they have shown what they can do. But in spite of this crossover, colleges have traditionally made a distinction between these two types of writing. "Creative" writing is taught in schools of liberal arts, and news and advertising writing in schools of journalism or advertising. Writing poetry and novels is considered an art and writing news reports and advertising copy a trade.

Recently schools of journalism have been christened with a new name: schools of communications. It is easy to see why. Prehistoric tribes communicated by speech and smoke signals, but after writing was invented, communication beyond voice range was mostly carried on by written messages. Until recently, newspapers did a large part of the carrying. Now, of course, daily messages are also carried by radio and television. There has been an industrial revolution in information and popular culture. More people are getting messages, and the messages are changing with the larger and different public, and with the greater distances and shorter time of message travel.

Communications has become an enormous industry, and communications specialists have been studying the effects of symbols on people. They have found that colors and sounds as well as words have a symbolic effect, often unconscious. Graduate schools buzz with talk about "the medium and the message": How does a message, image, or story evoke a response? How does a medium such as television create a common public across boundaries of space and social class? How do societies produce symbol systems? How can we set standards for communications acts and policies in changing cultures?

This book is not concerned with such problems. It is mostly concerned with the jobs open to young people in several parts of the communications business—newspapers, magazines, technical writing, advertising, radio and television, and book publishing. In all these businesses, the writer is the chief communicator, but he has many helpers in related jobs. We will discuss writing jobs, and such other jobs as are open to a young person with a general background in liberal arts. Jobs that require special technical training in accounting, printing technology, broadcasting electronics will be discussed only incidentally.

This book will not discuss free-lance writing, since this is a specialized field and requires a special study of markets and of techniques of producing and marketing acceptable typescripts. The format of movie and television scripts is rigidly prescribed and these scripts are almost always marketed through agents. Many good books are available on free-lance writing and marketing.

We will consider jobs in radio and television only briefly, since many of these jobs are much like the jobs on newspapers and in advertising agencies, and others involve free-lance work in scriptwriting and acting. Moreover, jobs on network dramatic shows are usually open only in Hollywood.

2

News Media

by
ROBERT ROTH

THE NEWS BUSINESS

Once upon a time there was a young person who wanted to become a newspaper writer.

She was steeped in the romantic tradition of journalism. She knew about John Peter Zenger, who had defied the censors. She knew that Thomas Jefferson had said he would rather have newspapers without a government than a government without newspapers. She knew about Richard Harding Davis, who became more important than the stories he covered, and about Ernie Pyle, who brought a war out of the trenches and into the homes of those who fought it. She knew about Nellie Bly, who went around the world for the sake of a newspaper story, and about Bob Woodward and Carl Bernstein, whose Watergate reporting forced a President to resign in disgrace.

The journalistic aspirant had, or so she thought, prepared herself well. She had a liberal arts degree. She had worked on her college paper and become editor of it. She had been a "stringer" for a paper published in a nearby city, reporting college news at space rates. In the summertime she had carried copy for a big city paper, and had learned to talk the language of newspaperdom.

She had prepared and sent to dozens of newspaper editors a résumé of her background and experience, properly confined to one side of a single page. Then she found that she couldn't get a job. It is a harsh fact of newspaper life—and has been for almost as long as there have been newspapers—that more people want to get into newspaper work than there are jobs to accommodate them.

Newspaper work does not pay as well as some other, perhaps less demanding lines of endeavor, and those who seek newspaper jobs know it. But the knowledge does not deter them, and never did. Neither do warnings that the glamour quickly wears off and is, in the experience of many if not most newspaper people, replaced by routine that offers little opportunity to break the big story, to expose the rascals, to clean up the city.

But every year a goodly number succeed in breaking in against the odds. Once in, they find that while their romantic anticipations may have been overblown, the practical advantages of newspaper work have been underrated.

SALARIES

Today's newspaper people cannot expect to become rich working at their trade, but neither do they risk becoming objects of charity. There was a time when the death of a veteran newsman was often the occasion for an office collection to give him a proper burial and to help his family until the widow could find a job. Now, thanks in large part to the Newspaper Guild, there are funded pension plans to take care of dependents, and the lifetime pay is comparable to what can be earned in other occupations. No newsperson can hope to earn anything approaching the roughly $300,000 a year that Walter Cronkite gets as a television newscaster, but the newsperson who does a good job can expect to own a home in a good neighborhood and send the children to college. And, if ambition should run that way, a newswriter can bear in mind that many of the most successful newscasters are almost without exception recruited, as Cronkite was, from the ranks of reporters for the written media.

QUALIFICATIONS, EDUCATIONAL AND PERSONAL

The first job is the hardest to get. The best way to get it, or at least the easiest, is to have a close relative who is an editor or a publisher. For the multitudes who cannot follow that route, however, some special qualifications are essential.

The first of these is education. In the old days—which were good or bad depending on how you look at it—a high school or even grade school dropout could walk into a newspaper office and often luck into a job as copyboy, running proofs and getting coffee for his betters. If he was brash enough and enterprising enough, he had a good chance to be given a tryout as a reporter. Many a successful newsman came up that way. Unfortunately, that way is no longer open. Most newspapers today will hire only college graduates, for the simple reason that there are plenty of these available and they need not settle for less.

Opinion differs as to whether the college education should include courses or even a degree in journalism. Some of the most outstanding present-day newswriters are products of schools of journalism. There are many others who have found it more useful to concentrate their schooling in areas outside the province of journalism schools. The skills taught in journalism schools, and the background knowledge they supply about many aspects of newspaper writing and production, can be and often are acquired by the working newswriter on the job. But a thorough grounding in history, economics, and political science, all important tools, is not likely to be gained after the job hunting has begun.

It should go without saying, but unfortunately it does not, that anyone who wants to be a newswriter should know how to express facts and ideas in clear, simple language. Colleges have graduated many who do not include among their skills the ability to write a simple declarative sentence. There was a time when some newspeople could get by without that skill, but they rarely got very far. Most of them settled into ruts as district reporters, telephoning local police and fire stories to rewrite men, and most of them ended their newspaper careers about where they began them. They are now a fast disappearing tribe. They flourished in the heyday of afternoon newspapers when the best and quickest way to get a story into the paper was to have the man on the spot phone it to an inside man who knew how to write. But afternoon papers do not dominate the field as they once did, and those remaining and prospering are tending increasingly, as are morning papers, to put less emphasis on speed and more on good writing which combines reportage with analysis and background clarification. For that kind of writing, the story can best be written by the person who covered it.

Writing ability is the first but by no means the only qualification required of a newspaper job hunter.

Also necessary is an insatiable curiosity, an unquenchable desire to know not only what happened and to whom and when and where, and also why it happened. A newsperson had better not be shy. He or she must have a certain amount of cynicism, of unwillingness to take anything at face value, and at the same time enough idealism to believe that the written word is a mighty weapon capable of righting wrongs and enriching lives. It must be remembered, however, that the editor doing the hiring will not know whether applicants have those attributes until they have been on the job a while. But the hirer will know almost instantly whether the hireling can write. It is helpful if the new person has some familiarity with newspaper style, but that is not a matter of grave concern, for new skills in that area can be quickly learned.

GETTING A JOB

Let us assume now an aspirant who is ready to seek a first job. That takes what tyros have always needed —time, patience, and perseverance. There are few shortcuts. One might answer a help-wanted advertisement in *Editor and Publisher,* the newspaper trade journal, and land the job. One might blunder into a city room just after someone has been fired or has quit and there is pressing need for a replacement. But such occasions are rare and are not to be relied upon. Most of the time the job hunter has no alternative but to keep trying until a job is landed.

This involves sending résumés by mail, and making the rounds with them in person, to as many newspaper offices as can be reached. Almost always the applicant will be told that there are no openings, but to leave a résumé, which will be kept on file for consultation should an opening occur. Usually this is nothing more than a polite way of getting rid of the applicant. There are, however, a few conscientious editors who really do keep a file of résumés, and who will, when opportunity offers, recall for interview some who have made favorable impressions.

In recent years another avenue of opportunity has been opened for college students who want careers in journalism. Most major newspapers, and a good many minor ones, now have summer intern programs. Students in their junior and senior years are given summer jobs that enable them to learn some of the fundamentals of newspaper work and that give their employers an opportunity to judge their capacity to become permanent employees. Internships are not easy to get. Applications should be made in writing, usually to the managing editor, and addressed to as many newspapers as possible, no later than February of the year for which application is filed.

Many have trouble deciding whether to seek the first job on a large paper or a small one, in the hometown or in the big city. A generation ago the novice would have been advised to start on a small paper for maximum opportunity to try many kinds of reporting and to learn more about newspaper production than would be possible on a metropolitan daily. That advice is still sound, but is not as universally subscribed to as it once was.

Some skills are more readily acquired on small papers than on large ones, and once acquired they are always useful. A good crime reporter in Ashtabula will be a good crime reporter in New York or Chicago. A good political writer in Yonkers can quickly become a good political writer in Washington.

Jobs on small newspapers are, on the whole, easier to get than jobs on large ones. There are fewer metropolitan dailies now than there were even a decade ago, and the number keeps decreasing as newspaper economics creates more and more one-newspaper cities. This fact should not, however, discourage ambitious applicants. The total number of newspapers has actually not declined very much.

What has happened is that, as inner-city circulations have declined and metropolitan dailies have merged, new, smaller dailies have sprung up in the suburbs. These suburban papers offer good, if limited, job opportunities. Most of them are prospering and pay good salaries, but only to a very few. They are good starting places for some, and for a few who are willing to stay in something less than the big time they can offer permanent and rewarding careers.

While jobs on smaller publications are easier for the novice to land, it is by no means impossible to go directly from college to a job on a big city daily, without serving an apprenticeship on smaller publications. This is especially true for those who have mastered some essential specialties in areas such as science and economics, or the more usual musical, dramatic, and literary criticism. The decade of space exploration created an almost insatiable demand for scientists who could report and explain in language that everyday people could understand. The dominant need now is for those who can cope with the "dismal science" of economics in a way that makes sense to the average reader. Those who can do that are apt to find employment quickly.

There is one area of newspaper work in which the jobs available often exceed the number of persons seeking them. Good cartoonists are a rarity and are always in demand. Those who have drawing skill and imagination can usually get interviews far more readily than writers can, and their chances of being hired simply by showing samples of their wares are considerably better.

Outside the specialties a reporter must expect to move up the hard way, to progress from covering minor stories to major ones, to advance from neighborhood meetings to the city hall, to the statehouse, to the national capital. It is a long road and not many make it all the way. No newspaper will make a foreign correspondent of a reporter who has not been tested in the local arena or who has not mastered at least one second language. And no newspaper starts a new writer as a columnist.

To get that first job, the novice will do well to try for a position on as many publications, large and small, as possible. Sooner or later will come a hard decision whether to grab the first job offered or to hold out for something better. There are hazards either way. The writer who turns down the first opportunity may wait a long time for the second one, and meanwhile may go more or less to seed, losing enthusiasm and self-confidence, finally becoming ready to settle for a career outside the field of journalism.

On the other hand, accepting the first opportunity may lose the journalist a better chance that might come along soon after. Taking the first job offered might wind up in a dead-end street, with little promise of advancement and little prospect for escape. Many years of experience in the news business inclines this practitioner, however, to believe that the rookie reporter will be well advised to go through the door that opens first. If you have chosen the news business, the sooner you get into it, generally speaking, the better your chances will be to move up.

BUILDING A CAREER

Many people who start at the bottom of newspaperdom remain there, or close to it. Many who begin as district reporters or stringers never get any farther. Many spend their lives covering a single police precinct or an obscure agency. But this applies primarily to the undereducated hack of yesteryear whose stock-in-trade consisted mainly of a wide acquaintanceship in narrow political circles, an instinct for the jugular, and a copper-lined stomach which enabled him to hold his liquor. Such people do not concern us here, for there is little place for them in today's journalism. For better or for worse, their place has been taken by men and women who are better educated and better disciplined, less flamboyant and more reliable. The day of the reporter who thought he could work better drunk than sober is long gone.

The man or woman who gets on a newspaper today can count on an opportunity to improve. It is unlikely that anyone would have been hired in the first place without showing promise of being able to move up. And if this capacity is not recognized by superiors as soon as it seems it should be, the writer can move on.

Newspapering is still a mobile business. Though many stay on one publication all their lives, many more divide their working careers among several. Many a copy runner, unable to advance on one paper because of starting too low, has been able to reach the top on other publications. Alvin Spivak, to cite one example, was dead-ended for years as chief copyboy on the Philadelphia *Bulletin*. He gambled, taking a job in the state bureau of the International News Service, an agency (now defunct) that offered long hours, low pay, and no prestige, but gave its hirelings almost limitless outlet for personal initiative. Within three years, Spivak was chief White House correspondent for United Press International. Later he moved into a profitable career in public relations.

News Services

News services are a fertile training ground for young reporters. They do not pay as well as newspapers do, except in Washington and a few of the larger cities, but they are great schoolhouses for instruction in basic journalism. News service jobs are won no differently from other news jobs, that is, by applying for them persistently and tirelessly. Once won, they may put the recruit in a rut, as a dictation taker or a telephone answerer, from which escape may be difficult. But they may also put a writer on the road to journalistic eminence. James Reston of *The New York Times*, one of the weightiest and most influential newswriters of our era, began his career as a sportswriter for the Associated Press.

Sports

Sportswriting has beckoned many to a newspaper career. More than a few have gotten a foot in the door by supplying local papers with the scores of high school football and basketball games or by reporting on college sports events.

Sportswriters include in their number some of the best and some of the worst writers in the news business. Some cannot function without stale clichés. Others can make sports events come alive and endow them with a vibrant life of their own. Some sportswriters move easily and with distinction into other branches of newswriting, as Heywood Broun and Westbrook Pegler did in their time. Others remain true to their first love, as Grantland Rice did in his day and as Red Smith has done in ours. There is no better prose appearing in American newspapers today than that which Smith puts into his *New York Times* sports columns.

Specialties

Most newspapers are glad to give a newcomer who has mastered the fundamentals an opportunity to try various aspects of newspaper work, so that they can determine where the new writer fits best. Criminal, political, and overseas assignments offer the most glamorous, but not necessarily the most rewarding, opportunities. Newspapers always need reporters who can handle health, real estate, social, financial, and consumer news. Quick promotion often comes to those willing to make themselves expert in those areas.

Copyreading

Copyreading is one of the most important newspaper skills. Those who become good at it are always in demand. It takes a special kind of know-how to be good at reading what others write, to spot errors, to eliminate excess wordage, and to write a headline that conveys the gist of the story tersely and accurately. It also takes a special temperament, in which patience and acceptance of anonymity are essential ingredients.

The copyreader will never have a by-line in the paper. The job is not as much fun as reporting, nor does it offer a chance to move about as much or to meet so many interesting people. But the copyreader will have much less trouble than reporters usually do in moving from one newspaper to another. A good copyreader can walk into almost any newspaper office, grab a pencil and go to work, for newspapers always need more copyreaders than they can find. It is among copyreaders, not reporters, that successful editors most often are found.

OTHER JOBS FOR NEWSWRITERS

The newspaper is not, of course, the only news medium. There are trade journals specializing in news of particular industries. And, most important of all, there are the electronic media, radio and television, to which more people now turn for news than to newspapers. To some, these fields will seem to offer greater rewards than newspaper work can provide. But the college graduate pondering a career should bear in mind that those who have been most successful in all those fields began their careers as newspaper workers.

Newscasting

This applies with special force to newscasting. It is possible for enterprising young people to break into the news departments of radio and television stations without first serving a newspaper apprenticeship, but that is not how Walter Cronkite, Eric Sevareid, David Brinkley, John Chancellor, and a host of other top newscasters got their start. All of them were writing reporters, and good ones, before they went before the cameras.

Newspaper experience alone will not make a

24

newscaster. Good looks, a pleasing manner, and ability as an actor and entertainer are indispensable assets, but a newspaper is still the best place for an electronic news merchant to learn the trade. Local radio and television stations recruit most of their news personnel from newspaper city rooms. Many an editor has been heard to complain that as soon as a promising young reporter reaches the point of being valuable to the paper, a radio or television station will lure that reporter away with more money than the newspaper can match.

Electronic journalism is only one of the callings for which newspaper work is the best preparation. The ease with which a good newsperson can move into other and sometimes more profitable lines of work is not the least of the inducements offered by a newspaper career. But before moving to these greener pastures, the writer should look over the opportunities that wait, so to speak, in one's own backyard, where the grass may be just as lush.

Newspaper people are prone to think that theirs is the best profession, bar none, and most stay in it for life. Franklin P. Adams once remarked that "any time you hear someone say 'I used to be a newspaperman once myself,' you know he never was." Adams, one of the most admired newspaper columnists of an earlier generation, could not conceive of a true newsman who wanted to be anything else. Nevertheless, many who begin their careers on newspapers find success elsewhere.

News Publications and Public Relations

Some newsmen move from newspapers to newsmagazines—*Time, Newsweek, U.S. News & World Report*—which, by and large, pay better salaries than most newspapers, but which, also by and large, offer

25

less scope for individual enterprise and expression. Some journalists go to work for newsletters that concentrate on special areas—economics, finance, postal service, meat, corn or oil production, Washington politics, or the like. These, except for a few giants like the *Kiplinger Report,* are small operations requiring limited personnel.

Some opt for public relations, either as employees of established firms or as proprietors of their own agencies, in which they try to capitalize (not always with success) on what newspaper work has taught them about making friends and influencing people. Modern industry has an avid appetite for men and women with newspaper backgrounds. All large business enterprises, and a good many small ones, consider public relations departments essential, and these are staffed almost entirely by people with newspaper background.

In all these and in many kindred fields, newspaper experience is, if not a prerequisite, at least a valuable asset. A young woman of my acquaintance had two years' experience as a Jill-of-all-trades on a newspaper and then went to work for a Washington-based research foundation, where she did well and quickly won promotion. A superior told her it was not her master's degree that made her valuable, but her newspaper training, which had given her an eye for the essential and had taught her how and where to look for what she needed to know.

Assistant to Politicians

Politicians have a special need for assistants with newspaper experience. Every senator, representative, governor, mayor has a former newswriter on the payroll. Every candidate needs at least one.

The most prestigious and probably the best-paying

political job to which a newswriter can aspire is that of press secretary to the President of the United States. With a single exception, every one who has ever held that job has had newspaper experience. The exception was Ronald Ziegler, who was not conspicuously successful as press secretary to President Nixon.

Sometimes newspersons move beyond being aides to politicians and become politicians themselves. John F. Kennedy was a newspaperman before he became senator and President. Adlai Stevenson was a newspaperman before he ever became a lawyer or governor of Illinois or twice the Democratic nominee for President. Warren Harding moved directly from a newspaper office to the U.S. Senate and the Presidency. Many others have found newspaper experience a helpful preparation for political candidacy at almost every level.

THE FUTURE OF NEWSPAPERS

Nevertheless, newspaper work is attractive enough for most people to keep them from straying into other fields. Some young people considering the newspaper profession as a lifework are fearful, however, that they may be entering a dying industry.

It is true that since the advent of television millions have lost, or have never even acquired, the habit of reading newspapers. It is true that people today are suspicious of what they read, and are all too inclined to say, "You can't believe anything you read in the papers," or "That's just newspaper talk." It is true that each year there are more cities with only one newspaper than there were the year before. It is true that many newspapers, harried by constantly rising production costs, are getting by with smaller staffs than were once considered essential. And it is true that technology now exists which can bring news stories directly from reporters' typewriters to home screens without having to pass them first through a printed page.

But it is also true that, though there are fewer papers than formerly, total newspaper circulation continues to rise in rough proportion to the increase in population. Newspapers can do things no other medium can do. They can provide, as nothing else can, an outlet for local news and local advertising. Those who doubt the need for newspapers have only to note what happens to a community when its newspapers are shut down by a strike. Business goes into a tailspin. The citizens do not know and cannot find out what's on sale in the stores, what happened at the meeting of the citizens association or the PTA last night, what's playing at the movies, or even what's on radio and television tonight.

The printed word has unsurmountable advantages over the spoken one. It has both permanence and clarity. It can help the reader understand what was only vaguely grasped by watching and listening to broadcasts. It can bring the reader up to date on news that may have been missed.

A newspaper is a lasting record of events at home and in most of the world. Without newspapers, historians would be hard put to ply their profession. Newspapers, even in the age of television, are an essential part of daily life—and likely to remain so.

SATISFACTIONS OF A NEWSWRITING CAREER

As a career, newspapering can offer attractions that other pursuits cannot top or sometimes even match. Job security is one such attraction. On most newspapers it is dependable. Once news workers have established themselves, have shown that they know their jobs, they can usually stay on that paper as long as they choose. In any event it is not likely that one will be fired summarily. That is not something that can be said of the electronic media, which can and often do fire even veteran employees at the drop of a hat—or of a rating.

A newspaper person can expect to earn a respectable, though not a luxurious, living. One can expect to find the work consistently interesting, each day offering a new challenge and a new satisfaction. One can expect to be envied by neighbors who work from nine to five at more mundane jobs, and one can expect to be respected by them, for although newspapers as a class are not highly regarded by the uninitiated, reporters for some reason are.

Most of all, newsmen and newswomen can look forward to enjoying their work. They will meet more people and know more about them than others ever get a chance to. They will see more places, have more contacts than others, and have less need to truckle to those in high places. Most important of all, they will be part of a living organism that is an essential part of the life going on around it.

Of what other business, trade, profession—call it what you will—can all that be said?

3

Magazines

by
JOHN A. McNICHOL, JR.

THE MAGAZINE BUSINESS

A massive dam is built in the Middle East that promises cheap electric power for thousands. A new rock group sells millions of records with a distinctive sound. An important new drug offers to bring relief to some cancer patients. Women's fashions will make a dramatic change.

These are just some of the subjects covered in magazines today. Whether the magazine is *Rolling Stone, Time, Vogue, Machine Design, Medical Economics,* or one of thousands more, each edition of each magazine can be a source of information and entertainment for millions. While television brings us news and information, it can do so only in an abbreviated way—giving us headlines and some details on a relatively few stories. Like television, newspapers appeal to a very wide audience, and so they can't cover items of special interest in much detail. And even books, which are written on specific subjects, take considerable time from inception to the time when they appear in paperback or hardback form. The answer for many readers, then, whether their interest is sports or nuclear physics, is the weekly or monthly magazine.

There are various types of magazine publications —trade journals, or business magazines written for a specific industry or specialty; technical journals, generally for those in scientific and professional fields; and consumer magazines, which appeal to the widest possible audience, the ordinary man and woman. Because there are so many publications, catering to such a wide variety of interests, they represent an invaluable source of work for the young person interested in an editorial career.

HOW A MAGAZINE WORKS

Whatever the type of publication—a popular consumer magazine like *People* or *Cosmopolitan,* a trade journal like *Iron Age,* or a technical journal like the *AIA Journal* (a magazine for architects)—all magazines share certain common factors.

They all reach their readers according to a prearranged schedule. Whether they appear weekly, biweekly, quarterly, or at some other interval, their readers look for them to come through the mail or arrive on the newsstand at a certain time. Because of this prescribed schedule, most editors (the men and women responsible for the written and pictorial content of the publication) and sometimes the publisher (who is responsible for all facets of the publication) develop an editorial schedule. This plan designates the subjects and even the articles they believe their readers will be most interested in over the next year. Depending on this schedule, editors will assign their staff or free-lance writers to prepare articles. Of course, when magazines cover swiftly changing events, like sports or news, long-range schedules are difficult to maintain.

While the staff of a magazine may range from two

persons to seventy-five or eighty, most staffs consist of an editor (sometimes called a chief editor or an executive editor), a managing editor (the person actually responsible for seeing that an issue becomes a reality), associate or assistant editors, copy editors, editorial assistants, secretaries, and typists. In addition, artists and illustrators will lay out and prepare the graphics for each issue. A promotion department encourages potential readers to subscribe to the magazine. If the magazine carries advertising, sales representatives call on industries and firms to solicit advertisements. Finally, a circulation department handles the thousands of subscribers.

All these people—and more—are behind each magazine you pick up at a drugstore or newsstand. And to make you want to read that issue, they try to put in the most interesting and informative articles. To do that, an editor will assign members of the staff or engage free-lance writers to develop articles that will make prospective readers want to buy that particular magazine. If it is a newsmagazine, the article might be the latest happening in the Common Market, or if a scientific journal, the molecular construction of a new drug. But whatever the magazine, there is always a story waiting to be developed. For instance, if a newsmagazine such as *Newsweek* or *Time* receives a tip on a new potential contender for the Presidency, the editor may assign assistant and associate editors and researchers to document the story. Typically, editors and researchers will act as reporters, interviewing the potential candidate, his colleagues and enemies, his family and constituents. The editors will analyze the candidate's past record, any polls indicating his probable strength with voters, and the impact of his candidacy on other Presidential contenders.

That material will then be sent from the field back

to the magazine's home office. There it will be reviewed and assigned to a particular editor, who will write the story of the candidate, his background and his chances for the Presidency. Other assistant editors and researchers will develop mini-stories, called "boxes" or "sidebars," to give additional insight into various aspects of the story. At the same time, facts will be checked to make sure that no inaccuracies occur in the final printed story. After the story has been written, the copy editor goes over the text for grammatical errors, spelling, and style. Curiously enough, many editors function as reporters and writers, with only the copy editor functioning as a true editor.

While the chief editor reviews the text, or copy, the article is also sent to the art department. There, artists and illustrators will develop the necessary graphics to make the story most interesting and informative to readers. They might go to a photographic library, or "morgue," to find old photos of the candidate, turn the poll results into easily understood graphs, or prepare illustrations in watercolor, acrylics, or other media. At the same time, they will measure and lay out the copy and graphics to determine how many pages the final article will take.

The approved copy is then sent to the printer for composition. The compositors will use a photocomposition technique to turn the typewritten manuscript into the typeface that you see on the magazine's printed page. Using a keyboard, not unlike that of a typewriter, they prepare long, colored "galley" sheets of the story. These galleys are then sent back to the editorial offices for review. The editor who wrote the story and the copy editor will read over the galleys for misspellings or other typographical errors (typos). These errors are marked and the corrections are written in the margin of the sheet.

33

After the typos are corrected and the galleys are approved again by the editorial staff, the story of the Presidential contender is printed with other stories, bound into a magazine, and delivered to its readers all over the country or the world. To produce such an article requires a great team effort and a rather special kind of person—an editor.

QUALIFICATIONS, EDUCATIONAL AND PERSONAL

Editors come in a variety of shapes, sizes, and personalities. Yet they all have certain similarities—curiosity about people and things, a respect for truth and facts, and a desire to tell others about the world in an interesting and informative way. Although one editor may work for *Glamour,* another for *Sports Illustrated,* and another for *National Geographic,* they all share a respect for the written word, and for the truth of what they report. Editors must be able to prepare copy—from interviews to final copy checking—against deadlines, while ensuring that the facts are correct and the copy is well written.

Most magazine editors prepared for their careers by working on school newspapers and yearbooks, reading widely, and keeping their eyes open to the world. While editors traditionally have majored in English literature or journalism/communications in college, many magazines, especially special-interest or scientific journals, look for scientists, engineers, lawyers, or whoever may possess the necessary expertise to develop a story and tell it. Some topflight schools for the training of future editors are Syracuse University, Northwestern University, the University of Missouri, and Colorado State University.

Compensation is varied and depends on one's experience, the responsibility of the job, the size of the magazine, and the magazine's location.

BREAKING INTO A FASCINATING CAREER

For those who seek an interesting and exciting career, magazine editing offers a challenging opportunity. If you are interested, study magazines and the way they present their stories; take advantage of school newspapers to develop your skills; and study subjects such as English, journalism, social sciences, and history which will give you a strong background for understanding a story and its implications. If possible, obtain part-time work reporting for a community newspaper on sports, school-board meetings, zoning, and some other topics. Editing is a very competitive field and you need all the experience and skills you can find. For those who succeed, it's a fascinating career.

4

Advertising

by
ROBERT ENSINGER

THE FIELD OF ADVERTISING

Every year, more young, ambitious, and talented people look to advertising for a career that is both interesting and rewarding. What is this profession that attracts so many?

Advertising means both communications and education. You, as an American consumer, are today one of the best-informed and best-served consumers in the world because of the competitive role that advertising plays in this country. Advertising is a multibillion-dollar-a-year industry that has helped create the high standard of living we now enjoy.

The advertising profession demands initiative, imagination, creative thinking, sound expression, and common sense. It's a hard field to enter. The beginning salaries are not much higher than in comparable fields. And the work is demanding. But the rewards are great, both in money and creative achievement, for those with talent and determination.

Outwardly, the advertising profession looks glamorous because it's always in the public eye. Once you are on the inside, however, you'll learn that good advertising requires a lot of hard work. And it offers many opportunities for creativity, talent, the art of selling, and management ability.

There are opportunities for writers, salespeople, artists, production people, and research workers. If you want to get into advertising, you must first determine whether you have the particular qualities that will help you succeed in some branch of the field. As in many professions, there are always more people trying to get into advertising than there are jobs available. That makes the competition keen. But there's always room for good people.

Advertising is a business that helps sell industry's products. Almost any enterprise that sells anything can use advertising. Manufacturers, distributors, retailers—these are the people who pay for the advertising which, in turn, becomes part of their selling costs.

Advertising helps sustain the mass production of goods. Without it, many of our industries couldn't sell on a mass scale. Ample production means competition, selling ability, and advertising—and better value for you, the consumer. Advertising has been a great stimulant in our striving for higher standards of living. No society can progress faster than the desires of its people. In America, advertising keeps us eager for the latest development of our rapidly advancing civilization.

Advertising people must, first of all, help sell goods. But they also have a great responsibility: to see that the force of advertising contributes to the common good.

HOW ADVERTISING WORKS

The businesses that employ advertising personnel may be classified in the following groups: (1) advertisers, (2) advertising agencies, (3) advertising media, and (4) advertising service and supply houses.

Advertisers are businesses that pay for advertising to promote the sale of their products.

Advertising agencies are firms that prepare and handle advertising for the advertisers who are their clients. They receive their compensation on a percentage (commission) or fee basis.

Advertising media include all the different vehicles of communication through which advertising is presented to the public in its various forms.

When you work in advertising, you work in one of the following kinds of businesses:

Advertisers

Manufacturers	Public utilities
Distributors	Miscellaneous national
Retailers	and local advertisers
Financial institutions	

Advertising Agencies

Advertising Media

Newspapers	Television
Magazines	Outdoor advertising
Business papers	Direct mail
Farm papers	Miscellaneous media
Radio	

Advertising Service and Supply Houses

Printers
Engravers
Typesetters

Lettershops
Equipment and supply
   houses
Miscellaneous advertising
   services

The work done by advertising people may be classified as: (1) administrative, (2) creative, (3) selling, (4) buying, (5) research, and (6) production. The most commonly known specific jobs are:

Advertising manager
Assistant advertising
   manager
Agency head
Agency general
   executive
Account executive
New-business person
Copy chief
Copywriter
Art director
Artist
Layout person
Media director
Space or time buyer

Director of radio
Director of television
Publicity director
Public relations director
Production manager
Production assistant
Research director
Research assistant
Space sales representative
Broadcast time sales
   representative
promotion manager
Promotion assistant
Direct mail specialist

You'll never find all these jobs in any one company. The greatest number of them exist in advertising agencies, which probably employ about one third of all the advertising men and women.

The *advertising manager* is found in the businesses of advertisers and advertising media. The advertising manager usually heads up an advertising department. Many times, especially in small companies, this is a one-person department.

In the business of a manufacturer or a dealer, the advertising manager directs all of the company's advertising. If the company does not have an advertising agency, the advertising manager may be the one who prepares the advertisements. Therefore, the advertising manager should be able to write copy, and should be familiar with art techniques, printing processes, and so on.

Most newspapers, magazines, and broadcast stations have advertising managers who sell advertising space or broadcast time to the advertisers. The "ad manager" is like a sales manager in other kinds of businesses. In media fields other than publishing and broadcasting, the individual in charge of selling is usually called the *sales manager.*

The *agency head* is usually a seasoned advertising person, experienced in marketing techniques, planning campaigns, and making successful contacts with clients. The agency head must be a good business administrator, especially in the case of large agencies, some of which employ several thousand persons. Some of the large agencies also have in their organizations general executives, not necessarily advertising experts, who specialize in such matters as finance and other aspects of business administration.

An *account executive* in an advertising agency has charge of the work done for the particular clients whose accounts have been assigned for supervision. An agency may have a number of account executives, each handling several accounts. Account executives must know the marketing and related business problems of their clients, and they usually rate among the most capable all-around advertising people in the agency. They must be able to write copy, understand the use of art, and plan entire advertising campaigns. They must have a clear grasp of the entire job to serve their clients properly. They should also be first-class contact people who can sell ideas and promote good personal relations between client and agency.

The *new-business person* operates at the management level to sell the agency and its services to prospective advertising clients. In many cases this person is the agency head. The job involves recommending campaigns that meet clients' marketing and advertising requirements and promoting the use of the agency's services by prospective clients.

The *copy chief* and *copywriters* are employed by advertisers, agencies, and media—wherever advertisements and promotional materials are written. They prepare the text, or copy, of printed advertisements and broadcast scripts, and this requires great skill in the use of words and ideas. Good copywriters are not only experts at expression, but must have an unusually good understanding of psychology. They must know how different kinds of people feel and think and react to various appeals. Good copywriting is devoid of exhibitionism, but attempts to stimulate buying action and idea acceptance.

Artists and *art directors* are mostly employed by advertising agencies, although there are also many free-lance artists and art studios doing art work for both agencies and advertisers. Advertisers sometimes employ staff artists.

The *layout person* makes rough sketches to show the arrangement of the illustration, copy, and other elements of an advertisement or a promotion piece. This work is one of the most important steps in preparing an advertisement or a promotion piece. The effectiveness of the whole creative job may depend on it. The skill and training required to do good layout work are comparable with those required of a good artist.

41

The *media director, space buyer,* and *director of radio or television* perform the functions in an advertising agency approximately indicated by their respective titles. The agency space buyer often not only buys space in publications but also purchases broadcast time and other media services. This person frequently is a veritable encyclopedia of advertising rates and has intimate knowledge about the relative coverage and advertising influence of individual publications, broadcasting stations, and other media. An agency's radio or television director plays an important part in program selection and production of the show to go on the air for the client.

The *publicity director* handles news about the company. In an advertising agency, he or she works to get publicity for clients of the agency. Keeping in touch with the agency's account executives and, frequently, with the clients provides information on all newsworthy developments. The publicity director must be able to judge news values the way editors judge them, and to prepare stories in a professional style. He or she usually knows many editors personally.

In an advertising agency or a large advertising department, the *production manager* and *production assistants* handle the mechanical production of all the materials necessary to produce the advertisements and related material. The production department deals with printers, engravers, mat services, and numerous other outside services. It's their job to see that everything is done on time.

Many advertisers and advertising agencies have research departments that obtain and analyze information needed for profitable marketing and advertising operations. The *research director* and *research assistants* must have analytical ability and be capable of scientific judgment. They should also know statistical methods and psychological reactions to questionnaires and interviews, and be familiar with sources of statistical data of all kinds pertaining to products, markets, and distribution channels.

The *space sales representative* and the *broadcast time sales representative* call on advertisers and agencies to sell them advertising space in newspapers and magazines and broadcasting time on the air. These representatives comprise one of the largest divisions of advertising personnel. It's a good place for the beginner with sales ability.

The *promotion manager* is responsible for promoting a company's business, although not necessarily for advertising as such. The promotion manager for newspapers, magazines, and broadcasting companies compiles statistics and information proving the value of the advertising facilities the company has to offer. This information must be presented in convincing form. The promotion manager also prepares literature and selling material for space and time sales representatives.

The *direct mail specialist* usually works in companies that sell their products directly by mail. Advertising agencies, lettershops, printing shops, and other service organizations sometimes use such a specialist. The direct mail person is usually expert in writing sales letters and designing literature to be sent by mail. Knowledge of selling by mail, how it can be applied, and what returns can be expected is basic.

The jobs described here require a considerable amount of experience and training. In most advertising departments, advertising agencies, and media organizations, however, there is room for beginners. There are also other jobs in most advertising operations in which a beginner may get valuable advertising experience.

QUALIFICATIONS,
EDUCATIONAL AND PERSONAL

A good general education can be a great help in preparing for an advertising career. In college, cultural subjects are as important as subjects in advertising and journalism. A good knowledge of English is particularly important, and education should also include such subjects as literature, history, psychology, economics, and sociology.

There are many degree-granting colleges and universities in the United States that offer courses in advertising. Many institutions offer night and correspondence courses for those who want to work on a job during the day or who have already completed a general course.

The following is a list of important advertising subjects:

Advertising principles	Retail advertising
Advertising copy	Retail merchandising
Advertising layout	Fashion merchandising
Advertising campaigns	Radio advertising
Advertising media	Direct mail advertising
Advertising production	Window display
Advertising art	Sales management
Lettering	Salesmanship
Advertising research	Foreign trade
Marketing principles	Public relations
Marketing methods	Business psychology
Industrial marketing	Typography and printing
Marketing research	Economics of distribution
Retail management	Advertising law
Newspaper advertising	Television advertising

You can't possibly study all of these subjects, but it isn't necessary to study them all. Your course selection will depend on what fits into your program in a particular school.

GETTING A JOB

How do you get a job in advertising? There's no easy answer to this question. A survey of advertising people will show that they got into advertising in many different ways. Here are some approaches you might take:

1. Speak with the personnel directors of large companies. A good personnel director can provide guidance and advice.
2. Register with employment agencies. There are some employment agencies that specialize in placing advertising, marketing, and public relations people in jobs. You can find them in the classified telephone directory.
3. Contact a small manufacturer, dealer, advertising agency, or printer. Often there's a better opportunity for a beginner to learn the business in a small concern.
4. In some cities, advertising clubs offer vocational guidance for men and women seeking advertising jobs.
5. Write letters to many different firms. This method is highly recommended, because you can cover a large field in a short time. Your letter should try to arrange an interview and to make a good advance impression.
6. Check the classified telephone directory and the advertising columns of newspapers and magazines when compiling a list of companies to which to write. You can also refer to the *Stan-*

dard Advertising Register, a directory of all important national advertisers in the country, classified as to product; and the Agency List of the *Standard Advertising Register,* which gives information about the advertising agencies. These directories may be found in public libraries in most large cities, and in the offices of advertising agencies, newspapers, and radio and television stations.

As we mentioned earlier, advertising is a very competitive field, and initiative is one of the most important elements in all kinds of advertising work. So you might as well begin to show initiative from the beginning—in finding a job.

COPYWRITING

Copywriting, in the opinion of most copywriters, is the backbone of advertising. Most printed advertisements depend upon text, or copy, to carry the burden of the message, and even those that rely chiefly on a picture or an illustration use copy to complete the message. And, of course, copy is also important in radio and television advertising.

Copy crystallizes the entire message of the advertisement or commercial and frequently suggests the pictorial treatment as well. It embodies the thinking and experience of advertising in saying those things in a way that will prompt the reader, listener, or viewer to heed the advertiser's suggestions.

We've already mentioned that good copywriters are masters of expression and must have an unusually good understanding of psychology. But what is it really like to be a copywriter?

First of all, it's a great feeling to write copy and see your words in print. It's an even greater feeling to know that your copy is doing a good selling job. As a copywriter you learn quickly that you're not an island unto yourself. You must depend on and work closely with artists, production people, typesetters, printers, and engravers to produce an advertisement or a promotion piece. It's imperative, therefore, that you become familiar with art techniques, layout and design, production and printing processes. The more you know about them, the better you'll be able to function in the advertising field.

In industry, a copywriter working in an advertising department may be required to buy art, type, and printing. Most of the people working in these fields are professionals, and a copywriter can learn a great deal from them. Never hesitate to seek advice or an opinion from these "pros."

You will learn very quickly that your copy is not sacred to others. Both in industry and in advertising agencies, copy must be reviewed and approved before it ever appears in printed form. It goes through an "approval cycle" which can sometimes have a disastrous effect on good copy. Everyone you meet will feel qualified to review your copy. In fact, many persons reviewing copy will begin with pencil in hand, assuming that changes must be made. Obviously, when copy has been "reviewed" by seven or eight persons, the original story line or theme may well have disappeared.

These are facts of a copywriter's life. Discouraging though they may be at times, the good copywriter picks up the pieces and strives to turn out good copy that will do the job it's intended to do and that the writer will also be proud of.

The copywriter in industry often has a more versatile job. Copy for a brochure, catalog sheet, product flyer, or instruction sheet may be required. Or a price list, envelope stuffer, or poster must be prepared. This person may even ghostwrite a speech for a company executive, prepare a slide presentation, write copy for a trade show exhibit, or do a news release. Working in a company's advertising department can be an enriching and educational experience. Writing copy, either in an agency or a company, can be a most fulfilling job, often paying better than comparable work in publishing. And it can lead to other interesting jobs in advertising and marketing.

5

Technical Writing

by
JOSEPH CHAPLINE

THE TECHNICAL FIELD

There is a broad field in industry for anyone capable of rubbing two or more words together and having them make sense. Indeed, in this environment such a person is like the one-eyed man in the kingdom of the blind, and there is a wide-open field for good writers on all kinds of technical subjects. The range of subjects is incredibly wide and varied. There is the typical progress report that describes the results of work done during the preceding month, week, three months, or some such interval on a development project, which might take as long as a year or several years. The progress reports are a record or diary of what went on during the course of the project. There are house organs that appear sometimes weekly, sometimes monthly, sometimes even daily. These periodicals try to help personnel morale, help sell certain products to be introduced shortly, or do both. There are patent disclosures that extract from engineers' notebooks the essential ideas that will eventually go to make up a patent application. There are technical papers for oral presentation at some convention or meeting, or for printing in a professional journal. These are only a few of the kinds of writing needed today in industry.

A technical writer is someone who can run in on a new situation, capture its precise details, and return to the desk to put them down on paper in clear, concise words, so that someone else who needs to know about the situation can quickly and easily learn all about it. The situation may be anything from what a new medicine will do for a patient (the writer in this case is working for a pharmaceutical supply house) to how a new program for a computing system functions and how to make the new program operate. The technical writer is the amanuensis of industry, the communication channel through which *the word* passes to all and sundry who must know the facts.

A good technical writer can be compared to the typical newspaper reporter, who must run to a new scene—an accident, a pronouncement by some official—and as quickly as possible grasp the import and prepare copy for publication. The main difference, however, is that the reporter does not in general have the same degree of accountability for what is put on paper. We all know that often the names of the victims are misspelled, and there is no guarantee that a given version of "Who struck John?" is the truth. The technical writer has no such latitude. Another difference is in deadlines. The newspaper reporter must meet certain exceedingly close deadlines, perhaps several each day. The technical writer has deadlines too, but they may be three or six months ahead of an assignment, and there is thus more freedom to work on copy until it is exactly right. Furthermore, this writer is subject to the typical reviewing process, in which the text is read critically by those in authority and presumably "in the know." Newspaper copy may receive little if any rewriting and editing, while technical writing may receive a great deal.

HOW TECHNICAL WRITING WORKS

Until recently, the process through which a piece of technical writing went was somewhat like this: The engineer or inventor may supply the barest rudiments of some copy. The technical writer fleshes out this copy into something more nearly complete. That copy, neatly typed, is submitted to the engineer for criticism. Often the engineer is exceedingly busy working on the device itself and keeps putting off reading the copy. Great patience is demanded of the writer under these circumstances. Ultimately the copy is read, and approved with corrections. Some of these corrections may stem from inadequate knowledge on the part of the writer, and some from changes that have actually been incorporated into the device since the draft was written.

So the writer returns to the desk with the changes in hand and prepares a revised or second draft. Then this draft too goes into the approval system. Finally a draft acceptable to all concerned is hammered out and is ready for publication.

Today, with the advent of computers, the whole process of creating technical copy has been radically altered. Although our age has been called the age of space travel, the atomic age, the jet age, it is really the age in which we made data a commodity just like plastic, or wood, or steel—the age in which we generate data, store it, modify it, retrieve it, and do everything we would do to any other commodity. We even think of "data" as a singular word, although it is actually plural.

In the plants of one large electronic equipment manufacturer the whole process has been put on the computer. When copy comes into the technical information department, it is immediately typed into the computer and printed in lines of 120 characters or whatever the line length of the high-speed printer may be. Each line is given a serial number so that references to the copy can be made by this line number and the position in the line.

Editing and correction are now performed, not by pencil and the old-time editorial markings, but by a computer change order or orders prepared by the editor. Scanning the printer output, the editor prepares the change-order list: LINE 19, CHANGE "24 VOLTS" TO READ "25 VOLTS." LINE 28, MAKE "AS IT WAS" TO READ "AS IT WERE." Whole paragraphs may be deleted or inserted. When the change orders are all checked and completed, they are typed into the computer and the computer makes the changes indicated, *including* a total readjustment of the line-numbering system. When the copy is reprinted, one cannot tell where any of the corrections were made.

The manual, or guidebook, or whatever the work is called, is retained in this computer form until final approval is given for printing an edition. The copy is then passed through an editorial run which breaks down the lines into the specified line length of the final publication, taking into account the variable type widths of the various letters. Most manuals are prepared in a two-column format with a certain line length, certain spaces between columns, and certain margin widths. The justification process makes all the right-hand margins come out as straight (flush) as the left-hand margins. One minor hassle is the problem of leaving space for illustrations. Work is now going on—and with good success—not only to make proper allowance for illustrations but even to cause the computer to draw the simpler line drawings.

In any event, the editing run prepares the copy for the "typesetting machine." This is no longer the old linotype, nor even necessarily the high-speed typewriters, although they are used in some smaller operations. Today we have optical typesetters that use whirling wheels or rectangular plates carrying all the letters and numbers of the type fonts. As the wheel spins around or the plate is scanned by an oscilloscope light beam, an image of each desired letter is focused on a sensitive piece of film. This film, when developed, can be placed directly over the sensitized offset master and converted by light exposure directly into the plate that ultimately is mounted on the printing press to print the actual pages of the manual. And the process of preparing the negative is carried out at speeds in excess of 1,000 characters per second.

Such systems are expensive at the present time, but with improved design and volume production their price will diminish, so that someday even smaller operations will be able to use them. The most impressive characteristic of this computer operation is that the copy is, like the bakery slogan, "untouched by human hands." Once the output of the high-speed printer has been checked and found free of error, all further operations are entirely machine controlled.

There is a final benefit to the whole system. Typically, a manual is issued under a certain date of publication. As soon as the device, or medicine, or whatever it relates to gets into public use, changes will be made. Adjustment procedures will be found inadequate, and there may be actual redesign on certain parts of subsystems. Corrections must be made in the manual. In earlier methods, the typesetters would actually retain the page setups in metal typeset "forms"—think of the weight alone! When in, say, six months a new edition was to be issued, the editors would provide changes in the copy, which meant new lines of type, new page layout adjustment, and new page numbering to bring the whole edition up to date. The computer system eliminates most of these problems.

A change can be entered into the computer at any time—one does not have to wait for the signal to prepare a new edition. The copy in 120-characters-per-line form can be kept up to date at all times merely by issuing change orders and entering alterations on the proper lines whenever it becomes apparent that some changes are necessary. When the time rolls around for a new edition, the copy is already corrected. It is merely sent through the editing run again and out comes the next edition, completely up to date. Pages are remade and renumbered, and nobody can tell where the changes have been made except by comparing page with page. This is the direction in which present-day technical writing is going. It doesn't eliminate the editor, it merely creates a new relationship between writer and equipment that can save much time and money.

QUALIFICATIONS, EDUCATIONAL AND PERSONAL

A Logical Mind

A technical writer has a logical mind. He or she should be able to solve puzzles with success and relish. A cryptogram, a crossword puzzle, or Martin Gardner's wonderful puzzles in the *Scientific American* are proper grist for the mill of the embryonic technical writer. One should have a good memory so that various ideas caught at different times and different places come together in the mind to form a totally new combination of ideas. At the same time, a logical mind forces the writer constantly to question, query, and doubt, until all possible doubt has been removed as to just *how* it goes together, *how* it works, *how* it is justified. The logical mind acts like a backboard against which an idea must be bounced. If it doesn't bounce back on target, something is wrong; something doesn't compute.

To begin with, a technical writer is something of a scientist; and a scientist, such as a medical doctor, a veterinarian, a physicist, a computer programmer— even a detective solving a murder mystery—is constantly extracting information from a reluctant system. What is a "reluctant system"? It is anything that has a logical order or organization, but whose order or organization is not known to the inquirer. Such a system is reluctant to divulge its inner secrets. It is unwilling to stand up and be seen in full view without some protective clothing. It is shy about revealing itself. It is the task of the detective, the doctor, the scientist, the technical writer to force the system to give up its secrets. This is where the methods of the detective come in.

A cryptogram is a simple example of such a system. How do you solve a cryptogram? (I speak here of the so-called simple substitution crypts in which each letter of the cleared message is given a simple substitute letter that is used consistently throughout the enciphered message.)

First you look over the whole enciphered message for familiar patterns. One of them might be "ABCDC," in which the third and fifth letters are the same. If you are an experienced solver of such puzzles, you at once see the possibilities of "there," "where," or "these." You then form a hypothesis or possible solution. From the position in the sentence, and sometimes with just a little intuition, you assume one of the three words and put it in the puzzle. Now there are other A's, B's, C's, and D's elsewhere in the puzzle and you are free to fill them in too.

But here is another word beginning in cleared form as "hte . . . ," and you know your hypothesis is not valid. So you go back and make a new assumption. The new assumption checks out in all places, and so you go on to a second assumption about some other letters, again checking with further extensions from it, and so on until you have completed the entire puzzle.

But there is one situation near the end of the puzzle that requires yet another technique. One word remains that has one or two letters that do not appear elsewhere in the puzzle. The whole message is cleared except for this one word. You must now resort to another method—context. You can, if you choose, try each remaining unused letter of the alphabet until you find some substitution that works. How do you know you have the right one? By context. You can say with certainty, "It makes sense! And no other letter makes as much sense."

Like the doctor faced with a new combination of symptoms or a detective faced with a new crime, the technical writer must decipher his subject so that the rest of the world can learn how it works. Perhaps the most frustrating and most typical question of the technical writer is, "But where can I find this material written up?" The answer is, "It isn't written up: That's your job!"

Sensitivity to Language

In addition to a logical mind with which to grasp a problem, the technical writer should be highly conversant with the language needed to explain it. The writer must be beyond the typical level where many who write through necessity and not through joy use their ears more than their knowledge of language to guide them through the complexities of composition. If such persons find themselves in linguistic waters too deep for them, they turn aside, rewrite, and come out with something they are sure of. They write around their problems and thus avoid some of the pitfalls, but not all.

A good writer frequently sits in a quandary wondering which of the five or more possible ways of saying something that spring easily to mind is the best way of expressing a point, while a poor writer merely rejoices to find *one* way of saying it. A good writer selects and chooses from a variety of means of expression, and is not restricted to a single means. Creation in nature is prolific; there is always a plethora so that the strongest of the species can survive. And in the good writer's mind there is also a plethora of means and a contest for the survival of the fittest. The task then is one of selection rather than of discovery.

A good writer should find the actual writing the easiest part of the job. I don't mean perfecting the text—that is hard work. I mean that a good writer can put words together effortlessly. The inexperienced writer is often so pressed for words that when they do come forth, they seem so valuable that to destroy, erase, amend, or in any way change them seems unbearable. A good writer tends to put little stock in the immediate product, the effort of creating it being so slight. Such a writer pays no heed to how much rewriting and editing must be done. The product has little value until it passes the writer's own discriminating and exacting test of validity. E. B. White, one of the great craftsmen of letters, has said that once he sat up until three o'clock in the morning working over a manuscript, and in all that time he was able to delete only one word, but it was worth it.

Technical writing is a craft, not a science. The process is akin to whittling—the careful removal of wood that is *not* wanted so as to reveal exactly what *is* wanted. There is a delightful story of the woman who came each morning to clean the studio of the man who carved the famous statue of Abraham Lincoln now sitting in the Lincoln Memorial in Washington. As the statue slowly emerged from the stone, the woman looked at it longer and longer each day. Finally one day she asked the sculptor, "How did you know Mr. Lincoln was inside that stone all this time?" The finely wrought text that describes some intricate aspect of technology is somehow preexistent in some as yet uncarved piece of writing. It's in there; all you have to do is remove the right pieces of "stone" to expose the real image in all its shape and precision.

The good technical writer should know the standard English that is the accepted language of fine publications such as *Scientific American, The New Yorker, National Geographic,* and *Saturday Review.* Perhaps the title of Theodore Bernstein's excellent book expresses the goal: *The Careful Writer.* Perhaps another name for it is sensitivity to words. A good technical writer has this. Like an insect with antennae reaching out ahead to sense what's out there, the writer's editorial sense of language is quivering in the current environment, always sensitive to poor usage or careless writing.

Let me give some examples. The word "transpire" means literally "to pass vapor through pores or tissues." Plants and animals both transpire (perspire). From this literal meaning a figurative meaning is derived, namely, "to leak out or come to light." Thus, there could have been a meeting yesterday at which neither of us was present. Today I ask you if anything has transpired from yesterday's meeting—a wonderful verb to have in the language. Yet the word has been browbeaten into a meaning completely foreign to that concept, namely, "to occur, to happen, or to take place."

Another example is the word "aggravate," which means "to make more grave." One can't aggravate something that is not bad to begin with. Yet how often one hears, "Oh, he aggravates me so!" Someone with a literal and sensitive mind can't help wondering whether the speaker is already a bad person who becomes even worse in the presence of the other person!

There are many more such violences that blur and degrade the language. A good technical writer is aware of them and avoids them.

In technical writing, the *subject* written about is technical, but the *writing* is not necessarily all dry fact. All writing—all communication among humans —seems either to arouse emotion or to convey fact, and except for some extremely limited examples, all writing partakes of both qualities. A love poem might be almost pure emotion—and so might a political harangue! At the other extreme, a doctor's prescription is pure fact. Technical writing is, we trust, grounded in fact, but sometimes gets off the ground. The progress report so common in industry is not without its emotional side. The person writing the report knows that the boss expected a little more to happen in that month than actually took place. The writing will take on emotional aspects as the writer tries to make what happened look as good as possible.

GETTING A JOB

What should a person do to become a technical writer? The field has hardly been in existence long enough to set many precedents, but there are some. Most directly, one can register at a college such as Rensselaer Polytechnic Institute in Troy, New York, which gives a four-year course for technical writers.

There are, however, many technical writers who have achieved their present status by far different routes. One, for example, is to study medicine, and rather than take the internships and qualifying examinations for practicing medicine, instead study writing also and become a medical writer. Michael Crichton, author of *The Andromeda Strain*, followed this route. In the reverse direction, anyone having a skill with language could study any of the many technical fields and become a writer in the field chosen. An example is Edmund Wilson, who wrote drama reviews and other critiques for *The New Yorker* for many years. When the Dead Sea Scrolls were discovered, his interest was piqued and he took off for the Holy Land, where he spent some time examining the scrolls, talking to experts, and becoming thoroughly familiar with the story. He later wrote a book, *The Dead Sea Scrolls,* which has taken its place in theological schools along with other "authorities" in this field.

Similarly, Kurt W. Marek was an amateur archaeologist and also a writer. He became aware that books on archaeology did not capture the romance of the field, and wrote, in German, *Götter, Gräber, und Gelehrter,* under the name of C. W. Ceram. It was translated into English as *Gods, Graves and Scholars,* and the author—to his dismay—has been cited as an authority in the field!

It doesn't make much difference whether one is first a scholar in a field—or an amateur, which means a lover—and then writes about it, or first a writer who researches a field to write about. Isaac Asimov has gone in both directions. He started out as a Ph.D. in chemistry, became a writer, and then researched and wrote about many other subjects—the Bible, the brain, the solar system, Greek and Roman history. His more than 170 books of course include superb science fiction. The basic requirements for a technical writer are to write lucidly and easily and to know a subject so thoroughly that one has something to say.

HANDLING A SPECIFIC ASSIGNMENT

These are the general requirements. In an actual writing situation, you would be given an assignment to go out somewhere in the company facilities to find a certain person who has been largely responsible for developing some new product or device for the company. This person, although thoroughly versed in the subject of which you must eventually produce the written description, is someone who is also extremely busy trying to get the device to work or to learn more about the new product, and whose time is at a premium. You may not, therefore, draw much upon it. What you must do is to get drawings, progress reports, patent disclosures, or any other document that may be available, plus any cursory conversation you get from the specialist involved, and go quietly back to your desk and start studying. Here is where your skill at cryptography will come into play. Whatever you get will be grossly incomplete. You want the documents that will tell you all so that you can write a document that will tell it all. Actually, the documents you want don't exist! It's your job to bring these documents into existence so that the next person, not you, can have an easy time of it.

You are now faced with incomplete evidence—a reluctant system. You may be tempted to run back to that specialist who knows it all and ask all kinds of questions, but you dare not—the specialist can't afford the time. Therefore you are put on your mettle to try to fit together, to extrapolate, to second-guess, to make coherent and sensible a lot of disorganized, incomplete, and even inconsistent material you have accumulated. You will be guided by your exquisite sense of logical consistency, your sense of coherence, and sometimes by just plain good guesswork.

Ultimately you may go back to the expert, but you may do so only when you have formulated a minimum of *golden* questions, not damfool questions. Anyone can ask a damfool question! A golden question is one that the expert will respect: it shows that you've done your homework and that you are able to understand a short and to-the-point response. The expert hasn't got time for filling you in on things that you could have found out for yourself if you had looked a little further. The expert can tell what you have or have not done with what you were given. You may uncover with a golden question something not even the expert knows the answer to. That happens! You want to get the expert's respect for your conscientiousness and growing understanding of the thing the expert has been working on for so long. The expert knows that your job must be done, but is loath to go back with you and rehearse the fundamentals of what has just been gone through and really, at this point, has lost its interest.

62

In time you will find the whole idea begins to jell in your mind: you can see how it all goes together, how it works, what it will do. You try writing on some aspect that you are most sure about. As these sections emerge, you can submit them to the expert and hope that time will be found to read and criticize your work—a most valuable effort if the expert will do it.

Little by little the full document takes shape. You may find that, after carefully crafting a given section, receiving some feedback from the expert, and trying to incorporate corrections, you are better off junking the whole thing and starting over. You must not be discouraged: this is the game of technical writing. It is demanding and exacting work. As we used to say when we were writing a manual for repairing a radar set, "Our audience may not be large, but if it is a sailor at sea with a broken-down radar set and the life of all on board depends on his fixing it, he is one of the most attentive readers a writer could ever hope to have."

If you are writing up the data on a new medicine, it is equally possible that a life may depend on your correctly discussing such topics as side effects, maximum dosages, and other medicines that might not be compatible with this one. The technical writer is an important cog in the information wheel. The world is dependent on you for correct and complete information, whatever the field.

Specification Writing

One field often described as technical writing is specification writing. It consists largely of picking up small parts—typically electronic—and describing them physically and electrically. They have a certain length and diameter and color and a certain number of pigtails for wiring into a given circuit situation.

Not only is this work dreadfully boring, but it does not really lead one into the true field of technical writing; it is a dead-end street. And those who seek good tech writers generally avoid the "spec" writer whenever possible, because so little is brought to the job of the real tech writer.

OTHER JOBS FOR TECHNICAL WRITERS

Suppose after some years you grow tired of being a technical writer, are there other jobs you might fit into? Yes, if you want them.

Patent Agent

One of the more lucrative jobs into which you may graduate is that of patent agent. Patents are the technical disclosure to the public of an inventor's idea. It is not a far cry for a technical writer in some development organization to pass to the position of patent disclosure writer. In this job you would examine the notebooks of inventors for possible novel ideas, and from them prepare disclosures that call the attention of the local patent department to significant inventions. (Incidentally, the novelty of an idea is not necessarily in its cleverness, but more in that it has never been patented before, so some knowledge of existing and prior patents is of help in this work.) In preparing the disclosure, you are preparing something closely akin to the main part of the patent: the specification. In this capacity you will probably be working closely with a patent agent or a patent attorney. Through this connection, you can become increasingly aware of the whole field of patent preparation and submission. You then obtain from the Patent Office in Washington a booklet entitled *Rules of Practice.* If you study this book thoroughly and go to Washington and pass a test, you can become a patent agent. This title permits you to do all the processing of a patent for an inventor, and even plead a case within the first court of patent jurisdiction (should such a case arise). You differ from a patent attorney only in that the attorney is a member of a bar (usually state level) and can plead a case beyond the first court of jurisdiction. Otherwise you are able to function as completely as a patent attorney in this field.

Advertising, Promotion, and Sales

Another move you can make from the position of technical writer is into the advertising, promotion, and sales fields. You may now be writing about the same products you discussed as a technical writer, and you will still be a word merchant, but you will not be under the demanding strictures of technical writing. You will now be writing about a product concerning which the facts already have been determined. Your writing will differ from technical writing in that the factual component will be smaller and the emotional component larger. Your task will be to make the products appear enticing, desirable, or necessary—or perhaps even to simplify the information so painfully extracted by the technical writer into a form suitable for the general reader. There are many opportunities in this area.

Scientist or Engineer

Sometimes you can move into a different kind of work in the technical field in which you have been doing writing. Some technical writers in the field of computing equipment, writing about how the devices worked and how to fix them when they stopped working, became so familiar with how the equipment worked and how it had been designed that they moved easily into the design area and later designed other equipment themselves.

Library Work

A way to step *into* technical writing as well as out of it is library work. Here the dual skills of librarian and technical writer enhance each other, no matter which is acquired first. Graduate-level librarians usually have a much better than ordinary knowledge of the rules of English. They soon acquire an aura of knowing lots of things, because they can retrieve information on demand. A simple question from a staff member to a librarian can evoke a large number of pertinent articles and references and the librarian appears to know it all. He or she doesn't really; what the librarian has is retrieval skill. It is not a big step from knowing how to retrieve information to knowing how to put it into good form for publication. In fact, it is a natural development from acquisitor of information to processor of information for publication. A route to technical writing might be via librarianship into editorship. The librarian/editor has two feet to stand on—a more secure footing than either one alone.

Editing

We have been focusing on writing, but editing is an area closely related to all writing. No writing ever emerges perfect and complete from the brow of the original author. It must always be gone over, fussed over, amended, redacted, and changed until it finally reaches a point where there is no more time available for further changes or—a rare state indeed—no further changes are needed.

Most writers do some editing on their own work. In some situations there are writers and separate editors who edit the writer's work. Newspapers have both writers and editors. It is possible that the product is better if two people work on it, depending on the skills of the people.

A good editor functions as a valuable auxiliary to the writing operation. You may believe you are writing carefully and in fact magnificently, but when you read the product in the cold light of the morning after, you may wish it would all go away and let you start over. The editor can step in at this dark moment and salvage the product. To return to the comparison of whittling, the editor can polish the sculpture the writer has roughed out, and possibly even change some contours.

The technical writer can move from creating text to editing the text of others. This is a fine calling and many have made great careers in it. There is some room today for the free-lance editor who can be called in by a given industry to edit one or more documents created by the technical staff that are not yet presentable. A free-lance editor may require some other source of income to tide him over dry periods. Editing is a good job for a married woman who wishes to spend time raising her children. The work can be highly rewarding intellectually and financially. Free-lance editing is a good way to eke out income from another source. (By the way, "eke out" is not equivalent to "squeak out." "Eke out" does not mean barely to get by; it means simply "to increase." One could make a million dollars a year and "eke it out" by taking in boarders.)

It may be a basic mistake to regard all school subjects as having equal value: science, language, mathematics, social studies. If the study of the English language could be pulled out from the rest and given special emphasis, even to the exclusion of some other subjects, students would have a tool for opening up any of the other fields and quickly comprehending them.

SALARIES

Salaries in technical writing vary widely with the knowledge and skill demanded, but on the whole are higher than for other kinds of writing. A beginning writer with a B.A. may serve as a copy editor and processor of somebody else's copy. A person with a B.A. who has some courses in chemistry or biology, or a double major in English and science, may rate a five-figure salary with a pharmaceutical company, depending on experience. Some jobs in the drug business require a heavy science background. Writing abstracts in biology or other sciences requires a major in the field and pays somewhat less than a job in industry. Public relations jobs in a pharmaceutical or other technical company pay about the same as other writing jobs in the company that do not require a heavy science background.

In engineering, the background required depends on the job. Technical manuals—for instance, on how to operate military equipment—are often written by technicians who understand the equipment but may not have a degree, only practical experience. The company may teach them how to write, or may have somebody else smooth out their writing. Manual writers might start low but could go up to a well-paying supervisory job.

A recent engineering graduate may start at a lower salary if he goes into technical writing than if he goes into engineering. Engineering writers who can explain complicated new research or sophisticated hardware such as that designed for space vehicles will make an excellent salary, as will writers who explain computer operating systems (software).

SATISFACTION OF A CAREER IN TECHNICAL WRITING

The work of a professional writer in the technical field is demanding and challenging. It can be intellectually stimulating and also downright boring. You have to take the bitter with the sweet. It is a profession that has its own being; it owes nothing to any other field. And above all else, it is vitally needed. The great institutions producing our technically trained people do not always do their job in also training these people how to express themselves easily and clearly. There is room for others to move in and take over this task of communications with the rest of the world. Sir William Osler said, "In science the credit goes to the man who convinces the world, not to the man to whom the idea occurred first." The technical writer has considerable status in the world, even if only by bringing some other person's idea to the world's attention. The technical writer might even inadvertently get the credit!

6

Radio and Television

by
MARGARET HARMON

THE ELECTRONIC MEDIA

Radio and television have much in common in the way they operate and the jobs they offer, but they also have important differences. Oddly enough, these two media have been exchanging places in the variety of opportunities they offer. This is because radio networks have been breaking up and television networks have been forming into enormously large organisms, with tentacles reaching all over the country.

The first radio broadcasts were made in 1920. Radio immediately swept the country; every town, every large department store, and every electronics manufacturer had its own broadcasting station, each putting out its own idea of a program. Then these stations began to form groups, where they could pool their money and put on better shows and so attract more viewers and more advertisers. Finally the coast-to-coast networks were formed. While each radio station used to employ its own writers and actors and announcers, now there were fewer jobs because so many of the shows were produced by the networks, hiring better performers and paying them higher rates but needing fewer people.

Then, in the late '40s television came along. It started the way radio had started, with little stations here and there. Each station was in fact a little theater employing writers, musicians, directors, actors, and stagehands. Budgets were modest, and shows were often on the level of high school plays, but there were opportunities for hundreds of people to learn the theater arts, which had now been transplanted almost intact to the new medium.

Television was so much better at presenting dramatic shows and sports events than radio that it soon dominated electronic broadcasting and formed the powerful networks we have today. Television took over the mass audience. Radio had to survive by breaking up again into local units and appealing to a "fragmented" audience—small groups of people with special interests, such as local politics, ethnic and foreign-language programs, country or rock music, and so forth. Television broadcasts are much more expensive than radio broadcasts and a commercial television station can't afford to put on a program for a small group of viewers whom advertisers won't pay to reach.

There are still radio networks and there are still locally owned television stations, but the balance has shifted. In 1954 there were about three thousand radio stations, but by 1971 there were seven thousand as radio became a local medium. Now, between 8:00 and 11:00 every winter night, more than three fifths of all American families will be watching television, and more than 90 percent of them will be watching the three big commercial networks.

The network shows are often produced on videotape so that they can be debugged before being broadcast and rerun indefinitely for added earnings. They are lavish and professional, and their writers, actors, and musicians are paid beyond the dreams of the people who used to put on a Western in an outdoor lot back of a local station. But, for most people, getting a job on a network dramatic show is just a dream. The majority of such shows are made in Hollywood.

It may be easier to break into radio than into television and the audience may be a little different. Commercial broadcasting is a business, designed to sell time to advertisers. The person who caters to a mass audience, whether an editor of mass-circulation paperback books or a writer of radio copy, should have some sympathy with and respect for the public. A desire to upgrade public taste may be praiseworthy, but the broadcast program that gives the public what is good for it, rather than what it wants, is likely to be tuned out.

HOW A BROADCASTING STATION WORKS

The breakdown of jobs in broadcasting depends on the size of the station. A small radio station may employ only four or five persons and the largest may employ over a hundred. In television the range is from about 30 to 250 persons. In a small station each employee covers several jobs—for instance, an announcer may also write copy and sell advertising. In a large station each employee has one special job. In practically all stations there are four departments—general administration, programming, engineering, and sales. The news department usually comes under programming, although in some stations news has been given its own department.

General administration covers the business management of the station under the supervision of the *general manager,* who works with the program manager, the sales manager, and the chief engineer in the day-to-day decisions at the station. The general manager sets and implements policies and handles relations with government units such as the FCC, and with the community. In a large station, this executive may have several underlings, plus a *controller* (or financial manager) who may also handle labor relations, personnel, and maintenance.

Some broadcasting organizations own several stations, which they supervise from a headquarters whose staff usually includes experts in law, labor relations, finance, and personnel.

The program is the end product of the broadcasting station. In a sense everybody works toward its production, but the programming department plans and produces it. Broadcast programs are supplied in three ways. They may be produced by the station itself, supplied by an independent production company, or supplied by a network to which the station belongs or with which it is affiliated. An affiliated station is independently owned but has a contract with a network to carry a certain schedule of network programs.

Most radio programming is produced by the station itself and, as we noted, the radio station offers more opportunity for writing and producing shows, although the station may also carry the shows of independents and a network. About one third of the radio stations in the United States are affiliated with one of the four national radio networks; others are affiliated with regional networks.

The networks supply the programs that are too elaborate or expensive for the local station to produce. These include practically all television dramatic shows.

The *local program director* works with the manager and the sales manager to set policies for programming. This director works with producer-directors and with talent to develop and improve programs and to decide which programs to buy from outside suppliers. Setting up work schedules and budgets are part of the job. The *production manager* works under the program director to handle the details of getting personnel and equipment together for a show. The *producer-director* is in charge of the actual production of a program in rehearsal and on the air. Selecting the performers and, in television, planning sets, lighting, camera shots, and music are the province of this maestro, who must be an artist as well as a good manager.

An important workhorse in both radio and television is the *staff announcer.* This job involves reading commercial copy, introducing programs, giving station and time signals, and making announcements. In a radio station it may also include selecting music to be broadcast, writing announcements and scripts, and operating turntables and other equipment. The announcer needs a warm and sincere voice, good diction, and a knowledge of grammatical and idiomatic English. On television, the staff announcer must also be attractive in looks and manner and something of an actor—not necessarily glamorous, just personable. Fluent speaking ability is important especially in radio where ad-libbing may be needed. A college education is not always a requirement, but it is important for advancement. A background in history, public affairs, government, economics, or the arts (drama and music) is useful.

After the staff announcer becomes competent, he or she may be promoted to the job of *special program performer,* part or full time. Here there is more money and more responsibility. Some become specialists—in sports, news, weather, farming, home economics, interviewing, or introducing talent in an entertainment show—and may handle production phases of shows, such as selecting persons to interview or public events to cover. The specialist must know the field. If it is farming, for instance, the specialist must keep up with local and national developments in agriculture, meet and talk with farmers, and speak at their meetings when asked. Programs might include sponsors who sell farm machinery or seed.

Ideally, the *farm director* is a graduate of an agricultural college and the newscaster a graduate in political science or journalism. The *newscaster* very often has experience on a newspaper. Broadcasting stations watch young reporters on the local papers, and, as soon as the reporters get some experience and show promise, may offer them more money to join the broadcasting station. Many other specialties in broadcasting require the writing of copy, and the person who can write well can fit into various jobs besides news.

The *sportscaster* may be a former sportswriter on a newspaper or a former athlete or coach. Sometimes a specialist builds up enough of a reputation to work free-lance for one or several employers.

Many stations have *news directors* who supervise newspeople and cover stories themselves. The *reporter* is usually the person who broadcasts the news on the air, and so must be able to write copy that will sound good, whether it is original or a rewrite of wire service copy. The *newswriter* may write and deliver an occasional editorial and may come to do this work full time.

In a television station, the *film director* screens and prepares all the film used in the station and helps decide which films to buy. The station may employ special *news camerapeople* to take film or still pictures.

Other personnel get and arrange props, prepare

cue cards, and time the show. *Graphic artists* design and build scenery and do other chores. *Dramatic actors* may be used occasionally, but most dramatic shows are supplied from outside. The *promotion manager* handles promotion and advertising for the station and its productions. The *continuity writer* writes sales copy for the sponsors' products and sometimes for a program, and handles announcements. This writer must be creative and imaginative, able to produce copy quickly on demand.

The engineering department creates the signal that carries the program out on the air and upon which the quality of the broadcast depends. A small radio station may have only a *chief engineer;* in a larger station, the chief may supervise ten or twelve *technicians.* A *television chief engineer* supervises from five to forty technicians. The chief has an FCC First Class Radiotelephone Operator's License, and may handle difficult repairs personally and advise on the purchase of new equipment. A technician who wishes to advance must also have a First Class license. Information can be obtained from the Federal Communications Commission, Washington, DC 20554.

Commercial broadcasting has only one source of income—the advertiser, who buys time for a commercial. The sales department must sell this time for all broadcasts. Stations get advertising through the networks, through national and regional placements, and through local placements. A network usually pays its affiliates for carrying the programs for which the network has sold advertising.

The *sales manager* of a station sets sales policy, develops sales plans and packages for special events and seasons, and supervises the sales representatives. The job may include helping to plan programs and actually handling sales to important customers, as well as writing their advertising copy. The manager must of course be personable, enterprising, and competitive. A college background is a help, particularly if the product is technically complex or otherwise special and the sales representative can act as consultant. Some stations prefer persons with experience in an advertising agency. The sales manager is the person most likely to rise to general manager.

The *traffic manager* must know all the activities going on in the station and make schedules to keep them on track without any collisions or late arrivals. An important duty is to keep a schedule of unsold time for the sales department. The job requires at least a high school diploma, and business education is an asset.

Networks have basically the same jobs as local stations, plus some special ones. Network production requires producers, writers, musical directors, scene designers. Performers—actors, singers, dancers—are usually hired as free-lancers. Network news and public affairs departments cover national and international news and special events for their affiliated stations and employ foreign and domestic correspondents, commentators, and newswriters. Network sales representatives deal with large companies and their agencies on nationwide campaigns. Network engineering requires top-grade people who can handle and even design advanced equipment. Networks need legal and financial staffs to handle agreements with their affiliates. Network jobs are often very good, but the competition is very keen.

GETTING A JOB

One way to get a job in broadcasting is to have experience in some specialty the station requires—

newswriting, advertising, sales, sports. Another way is just to keep trying and take any job open to get a foot in the door, and then learn from the inside. To be successful in broadcasting, at the network or any level, you must be a self-starter, able to think creatively on the job, able to work on a team, and able to work under the pressure of the relentless schedule of broadcasting. You must accept the fact that broadcasting depends on the public for its audience and on advertisers for its income, and must relate to both groups.

Broadcasting is a tremendous business—every year advertisers spend over three billion dollars to buy time. It is also a tremendous and vital social force. Anyone who works in broadcasting is part of that force.

7

Book Publishing

by
MARGARET HARMON

THE BOOK BUSINESS

At first glance it might seem that publishing books is just an extension of the business of publishing newspapers and magazines, and that the jobs would be much the same in all three. But there is a difference. Newspapers and magazines are sold by subscription, or on newsstands where the buyer knows what to expect in the general content of the publication and the price. Forecasts can be made about sales and profits, based on market studies and economic factors.

A publishing house, however, is in a sense a whole collection of enterprises. Every book is a new and separate product, separately conceived, designed, and manufactured under a separate contract with each author. There is no sure way of estimating its sale, especially if it appeals to a mass market. Magazines like *National Geographic* or *Playboy* can count on a certain customer loyalty, and so can automobile manufacturers even if they make design changes. But few people know who publishes the books they read, and readers develop a loyalty to only a few popular authors. Textbooks and scientific books are not quite so much of a gamble, since they have a definite market.

Because a lot of toil, tears, and teamwork must go into the planning and production of each book, each person on the team must assume a share of responsibility for the profitability of the book and must understand how his or her work affects that of the other members of the team. The primary business of book publishing is not writing—which is done by free-lance writers—but editing and processing the writing of others. The editors in the lower ranks, who fix up copy and prepare it for the printer, are concerned only with editing. But the senior editors are also the purchasing agents for the publisher—they pick out the books to be bought and have a say in decisions about their design and production. A senior editor must understand not only the literary qualities of a book but also the market in which it must compete and whether it can be produced at a reasonable price for this market.

The editor in a publishing house, if he or she wants to move up, must know a good deal about the whole operation. Many beginners get into editing sideways by first taking a job in contracts, subsidiary rights, or marketing. Some publishers permit an employee to switch from department to department to find out where he or she fits best, or move newcomers from department to department as a means of training. An editor will be a better editor for having had some experience of how a book is produced, and a production man will be better for knowing what the editor is up against.

HOW BOOK PUBLISHING WORKS

A publishing house usually works for a definite segment of society or a definite institution. It publishes religious books for churches; textbooks for schools; research for universities; books for doctors, lawyers, or businessmen; books for children; or books for the general reader. Educational publishing is the largest single market for books and probably the most influential kind of publishing.

A young person contemplating a career in publishing may dream of being an editor entertaining a famous author at an expense-account lunch. The odds, however, are heavy that the editor will not be dealing with best-selling novelists, but with the writers of schoolbooks or technical books. For every editor who deals with the novelist, at least twenty work on high school science textbooks. These twenty are unsung heroes—as William Jovanovich notes, everyone has heard of Maxwell Perkins, but who knows the name of the editor of the *Dictionary of American Biography* or Paul A. Samuelson's *Economics?* For that matter, who knows the author and editor of the *Auto Repair Manual,* published by Chilton? Yet this book makes best-seller lists look foolish. It sells over 400,000 copies a year, has been selling for years, and shows no signs of drying up.

Schoolbooks require more people and money to produce and sell them than do "trade" books, or books for the general reader. A textbook house with annual net sales of $25,000,000 from school textbooks will employ about 75 editors and copy editors and a sales staff of 120, while a trade publisher with half that sale can get along with only a fifth as many editors and sales representatives.

Even the largest publishing houses don't publish everything from Bibles to comic books, but carve out segments of the market as their own. They usually have separate departments for each segment—trade books, medical books, schoolbooks. Obviously anyone entering the publishing business on the editorial side should expect to wind up in some field with which he or she has an affinity, by interest and education.

Each publishing house has a characteristic style, depending partly on the kind of books it publishes. It has a literary and editorial style, a style in book design, advertising, and marketing, and a style of dealing with its authors and booksellers. This style is often set by the publisher if this person has imagination and force. A publishing house may indeed be the lengthened shadow of one person—or, in the case of Harper's, the shadow of the four brothers who founded the business and controlled it for decades. The Lippincotts, William Randolph Hearst, and Henry Luce are other publishers with long shadows.

A definite image is an advantage to a publishing house. It lets prospective authors, merchants, readers, and employees know what to expect. An image attracts authors and employees who fit in with it, and who in turn reinforce and develop the image.

DEPARTMENTS IN A PUBLISHING HOUSE

The division of the publishing business into separate functions—editing, design, production, printing, accounting, often carried out in different locations—is relatively new. When modern publishing began in the eighteenth century, the publisher was primarily a bookseller. The books were printed at the back of the shop and sold at the front. The printer-bookseller began by choosing a likely author to publish and getting this author to recommend other authors. But when typesetting and printing became mechanized, publishing and printing were separated, and other functions, too, gradually became separate operations.

Editing

The early bookseller-publisher accepted or rejected manuscripts for publication, possibly with the advice of experts. He suggested changes to the author if he wanted them. But the editing function gradually became a specialty, and today has become several specialties.

The "first reader" has the weary job of plowing through the piles of typescripts that the mail brings to the publisher in a never-ending flow. In 1965, Harper's received 6,355 unsolicited typescripts. As more and more people write books, some publishers, of both books and magazines, have begun refusing to read unsolicited material and will look only at typescripts submitted by agents, writers they know, or writers whose typescripts they have agreed to see after inspecting a preliminary outline and sample. They have been forced to eliminate the enormous cost of inspecting so many. Unsolicited movie and television scripts are almost never accepted, but are returned unopened for fear the author may sue the company for plagiarism.

Publishers tend to hire recently graduated English majors as first readers, since they are supposed to have the eagerness and stamina for the work. They are trained to pick out from the slush pile not merely what might appeal to their professors but what might appeal to the mass market which includes grocery clerks and truck drivers.

One function of the literary agent is to serve as a first reader, and to pass on to the publisher only typescripts that have some worth. Some agents don't bother to perform this function, but simply pass on to the publisher most of what the authors offer them, in which case the first reader might be called upon to screen such agents' submissions. But as a rule typescripts from agents bypass the first reader and go on to a senior editor.

The first reader returns typescripts believed to be hopeless for publication by his house because of subject, quality, length, or other characteristics. Those that have some merit are passed on to a senior editor, with a report appraising their good and bad points.

The specialization of the editorial function depends on the size and setup of the firm. In a company that publishes only a handful of books a year, one editor may do the whole job, from first reading to editing for the printer. This person may also be the publisher, or the publisher may be the person who goes out and scouts for authors. But a large company has a number of levels of editing. At the top are the *editor in chief* and perhaps other *senior editors,* sometimes called *acquisition editors.* These people are like the buyers in department stores, in that they understand the marketplace and the goods offered. They are entrepreneurs who are supposed to scout for quality merchandise. They have to be good judges of writers and their potential, as well as of scripts. Senior editors don't just sit in their offices and wait for scripts to come in; they go out and beat the bushes. Typescripts are the lifeblood of a publishing house. The house must have an adequate flow of publishable scripts to maintain the output it has set for itself, whether this is 25 or 250 books a year. If the house is geared for 250 and gets only 200, it will be in trouble because salaries and overhead will continue, and it will have to cut back expenses in a hurry or go bankrupt. In such an emergency the house tends to lower its standards just to keep up the level of output. The more scripts it has to choose from, the more selective it can be, and the better it can conform to its image.

Keeping up this flow of typescripts is the business of the senior editors. An editor keeps in contact with authors the house has already published, by letter, phone, or personal visit, and asks about their next books. The editor talks to agents. In fact, agents too scout around for new authors, think up ideas for books and find writers to write them, help the author shape up the book, and negotiate for subsidiary rights as well as the initial sale.

A senior editor who is a specialist in some subject such as medicine or law reads professional journals, looking for possible authors and keeping up with what is going on in the field, making friends with professionals and asking them to recommend authors, and developing contacts with university departments in the specialty.

W. B. Saunders, the largest health-science publishing house in the United States and perhaps in the world, publishes some 150 new books a year, with a backlist of at least 500 titles. It doesn't depend on—or in fact want—unsolicited typescripts. It looks for a void in an area of its specialty and seeks out an expert who can write a book to fill the void. It gets queries and scripts from medical professionals, but seldom publishes these "over the transom" entries.

It can be seen that the editor is sometimes the creator of the book, thinking up the idea and procuring the author. The editor may also edit the book before it is written: when a book in outline or unfinished form comes in, the editor discusses its organization, style, most promising market, and illustrations with the author, and may largely shape up the project. The editor is not a dictator, but an informal and helpful person on whom the author may come to rely as a friend. Great editors are sometimes as responsible for great books as great authors are. The editor can of course also shape up and condense a finished script, as Maxwell Perkins did to the amorphous literary outpourings of Thomas Wolfe. All this work with authors is justified because a publisher wants *repeat* authors who will keep sending in scripts and build up a following, and it is worthwhile to help an author write better and improve output.

It is in this contact with authors that the born editor gets the greatest satisfaction, a sense of being a creator. But editors must know where to draw the line. They must not try to take over a script and make it their own. They should not be failed authors who try to be writers themselves at second hand. They must be like teachers or coaches, guiding an artist from behind the scenes and sharing anonymously in the triumph. They must relate to each author with tact and sensitivity. They must understand the author's idea of the book, the dream; and of course understand the readers' dreams and unconscious needs, too, in order to match them in a selling book.

A senior editor, on getting a typescript from a first reader or from an agent, may decide to reject it or to recommend it for publication. If unsure about it, the editor gets other people to read it. Very bad and very good books present no problem; the ones in between do. Unfinished books, for which the author has submitted only an outline, or an outline plus sample chapters, are special problems. The subject may be very attractive, but the finished book may not live up to expectations, especially if the writer's performance is not known. Yet if the editor doesn't take a chance on it, some other publisher may; and if it turns out to be a best-seller, the editor's reputation will suffer. However, all editors make mistakes, and as one publisher told a woman editor who had rejected a best-seller, the books to worry about are the ones accepted, not the ones that got away.

The senior editor, on deciding favorably about a typescript, confers with the author on the contract terms and revisions. The editor then prepares to present the script to the publisher, talking with people in the design, production, and marketing departments, getting opinions and estimates, and drawing up a budget. If it is a technical book, the script goes to an outside expert for appraisal. Other books on the subject are checked to see how well they have done and whether the subject is already well covered.

Of course, this procedure is shortened if the book was solicited by the publishing house and nursed along by the editor while it was being written.

Books sponsored by senior editors are presented at a meeting of the editorial committee. This committee meets often—perhaps every two weeks. It usually includes the publisher unless the company is large, in which case it includes the head of the division. Other members are the marketing manager, the editor in chief, the editors who are sponsoring typescripts, and perhaps other editors as well. The design and production departments have already supplied estimates. If the project is large and expensive, the chief financial officer also attends. The final decision is of course the publisher's.

If a book is obviously a valuable property with mass market appeal, the publisher may explore possible reprinting by a paperback publisher and get a commitment before deciding to accept the book. Accepting a book by a top popular author requires an enormous payment—a hundred thousand dollars or more, perhaps—to the author and agent, and income from subsidiary rights will be needed to justify the gamble. Major books are often auctioned off among publishers. The agent may send a copy of the script to every likely publisher and ask for bids. The money paid by the publisher is a guarantee or nonreturnable advance against royalties. Even nonfiction books may cost as much as $25,000. These high fees are a recent phenomenon. Payments for the average good book of fiction or nonfiction have no more than doubled in the last ten years, to about $15,000, and a first novel brings $2,500 or less. Children's books bring much smaller advances. Auctioned books often fail to earn the guaranteed advances, and prices may soon come down to more reasonable figures.

After the book has been formally acquired and the contract signed, the next level of editing takes place. This may be done by the same editor who secured the book or by another editor, depending on the size and organization of the house. The process is called copy-editing or sometimes production editing.

Copy-editing

A copy editor checks over the details of writing— grammar, punctuation, structure, reviewing the whole typescript for content, consistency of style, and appeal to readers. A list of proper names in the script and other words about which there may be a choice in spelling or capitalization is made and consistency of usage is stressed. The copy editor makes notes, either separately or in the margins, of suggested changes. Sometimes changes can be made immediately; sometimes the author must be consulted. Some authors welcome help from an editor and some resent the change of a single one of their golden words.

A good copy editor can take a carelessly and awkwardly written typescript and turn it into a professional product with a good chance of sale. Picking up errors in fact or grammar can keep the author from looking foolish and getting tons of letters pointing out mistakes. The copy editor can make or break a book, and cement or rupture the house's relationship with an author. Though not an expert on the subject of the book, he or she should know where and how to check facts on anything. A true skeptic, the copy editor will verify everything about which there is the least doubt. Young English majors are often given the job of copy-editing, and may feel relegated to what they consider to be a dreary routine. They should, however, welcome a copy-editing job as fine training in concentration, attention to detail, and research. The copy editor acquires a great deal of knowledge and taste unconsciously, by a kind of osmosis.

The copy editor is supposed to prepare the typescript for the printer. The script may or may not be returned to the author for approval or changes. By this time the script may be a nightmare for the compositor. As Robert Landau's book on computer composition notes: "Words and sentences are now crossed out in one color, marked 'stet' in another, additions are written in longhand, and directed with graceful loops or arrows to their proper places; paragraphing is changed, and slips, marked Insert A or No. 1, are clipped or stapled to the pages." Copy this poor may have to be retyped. This will happen increasingly when the input must be readied for automatic photocomposition.

In disputes between the author and the publisher or the editor about changes, who decides? Legally if not in fact, the author under contract is the equal of the publisher. The contract requires the delivery of a completed typescript, ready for the printer. The publisher may want to do minor editing and make changes in the text, but the author has the last word.

Traditionally, the author is obligated to read proof. Proofreading is a part of quality control and is done to ensure the correct typesetting of the copy. It also offers the author a tempting opportunity to make improvements in the book, but these author's alterations, or "aa's," are expensive. The publisher will pay for only a minimum, and the author must pay for the rest.

Proofreading

Proofreading is also a valuable means of training in concentration and the conventions of printing. It is how some important people in the book business learned their trade.

The proofreader compares the typescript, or copy, with the printed proof and marks all mistakes the printer has made in copying the text, in using the wrong font, in not aligning the type properly, in indenting or spacing incorrectly, and so forth. There are standard symbols for such corrections. Further, the proofreader is not supposed to let a mistake in spelling or grammar go by, even if it was made in the original script. If the copy has not been edited fully, the proofreader's task is much more difficult. One must be alert for errors and exercise careful judgment in weighing the cost of change against the values of accuracy and appearance. Like the copy editor, the proofreader should keep a memorandum of the choices made and see that they are maintained consistently.

Proofreading is sometimes done by two people: a reader reads aloud from the proof and a copyholder follows the original. This system, however, is not practical in reading mathematical equations or foreign languages the proofreader does not understand. A proofreader who works alone compares the proof with the copy word by word or even letter by letter. Whether one or two persons are used, there should be a second silent reading of the printed proof without reference to the copy to check the sense, style, and appearance of the page. It is the proofreader who may catch that last mistake that got by the copy editor, and make the book perfect.

The first proofreading is done by the compositor's proofreaders. Notations are marked on a master proof, which includes queries carried over from the copy. The master proof and a duplicate are sent to the publisher, who sends the duplicate to the author, perhaps with the queries. The copy and the master proof, incorporating author changes, are sent back to the compositor. Some publishers have their own proofreaders, others rely on the compositor's staff. After the compositor has corrected the type, a new proof is pulled, which must be checked to see that the corrections have been made properly—and that no new errors have been introduced in resetting lines or parts of lines.

Proofreading may in fact become obsolete within a few years. Input tapes for composing machines have long been made with typewriter-like devices that not only record on the tape but also produce printed or "hard" copy, so that the record on the tape can be checked for errors. Until recently it was difficult to correct errors on the input tape, but this is no problem with computer composition. Errors can simply be fed into the computer in sequence. The computer then generates a correction tape and merges the corrections with the original tape, including deletions, additions, and shifting of copy. The merged tape is then fed into the photocomposing machine. Errors introduced by machine in computer photocomposition are negligible, and there is no more need for checking the output than there is for checking the output of a computer.

For computer composition, the author must make all changes on the original typescript, since there will be no opportunity to read proof after seeing how the text looks in print. However, there *will* be more time to retype and revise copy, since the elimination of the proofreading cycle and the great speed of photo-composition will shorten the time needed to produce the book.

Design

When we pick up an ordinary book, we don't think of it as having been designed; we suppose that somehow it just happened. But before it could be printed and bound, somebody had to sit down and decide what it was going to look like—the kind and size of paper and type, width of margins, layout of the title page and other special pages, type of binding, and size and method of reproduction of any illustrations. Art must be created for the book jacket or the cover of a paperback book. The book designer must make a book that will hold together, and be easy and pleasant to read, within the budget set for its production. A good book designer makes an attractive book, and sometimes a beautiful book.

The designer is also an expert in typography, or in choosing appropriate typefaces and sizes for a book and arranging the type and space to aid the reader's comprehension of the text. Sometimes, as in advertising copy, typography is used as a means of getting attention or creating an emotion.

The designer is related to the production manager much as the architect is related to the builder. The architect draws up plans for the details of the building, which are integrated into a pleasing, functional design. To do this the architect must know all about the materials and processes used in construction, including their relative cost in the locality, in order to design the best building for the money available.

The book designer must also know about the processes that go into bookmaking and what facilities the publisher has or can procure for illustration, composition, printing, and binding. A design must be matched to the press available, or a press must be found to match the design. A slight increase in page size or margins could greatly increase the cost of a book. Planning a book for a rotary instead of a cylinder press, on the other hand, might lower the cost considerably, especially if binding operations are integrated with the press. In planning the reproduction of illustrations, the designer must know the relative qualities of plate materials and platemaking techniques, and select the most efficient and economical ones.

The role of the book designer has changed as printing technology has changed. The designer used to be concerned mainly with the appearance of the book, but now he or she has much more to do with the economics of production and with making the unique business venture which is the production of this book a profitable one.

Photocomposition has given the designer a lot more leeway in laying out and dressing up pages. When hot type is cast on metal slugs, it is very difficult and expensive to break up a page of type to insert illustrations or other irregularities. In photocomposition, however, changes are just a matter of cutting and pasting film.

The designer works not only with production people on the output end, but also with the author and editor on the input end. The designer must understand the author's concept of the book and develop a vision of the finished book that conforms to and enhances this concept. The design may bring out the very essence of the book, be it a children's fairy tale, a book of science fiction, or a book on archaeology.

Of course, not every book warrants expensive design and illustration. The budget of a mass market paperback, for example, does not usually include a large amount of money for design.

However automatic book production may become, there will always be need for the designer. Attractive book design is more important than ever, since books now have to compete with visual media such as movies and television.

Typographic design may change with photocomposition, and the designer will have to adapt to the changes, even if asked to design a contoured lap reader for microfilm and a typeface easy to read with a magnifier.

Production

The production department takes the text produced by the author and the editor, and the instructions for format drawn up by the design department, and turns them into a book. However, the production manager does not wait until these items arrive in the office to give attention to the book. He or she works on the book from its very beginning, even before the typescript is accepted, by providing cost estimates, discussing problems in manufacture, and helping to draw up plans and a budget for the book.

In small houses the production department may do the design, and in houses of any size the design department may be supervised by the production manager. A duplicate may be given to design and production before the typescript is edited so that they can be working on it. Production may advocate the policy of standard designs for series and for certain types of books, and standard trim sizes for the house and even for the industry. Books that are run in the same size can be "ganged up" or run in sequence without expensive paper changes and adjustment of the press.

Few publishers maintain their own printing plants. Even when a big house has its own plant, it is operated as a separate unit and other divisions of the house purchase printing from it. But even a printing plant dedicated to one publisher may have to buy printing outside at peak periods. Most publishers find it more efficient to buy printing and binding from a number of outside suppliers. The production department deals with these suppliers, getting estimates, letting contracts, scheduling and routing proofs, checking invoices—a kind of traffic manager.

Even a small publishing house may have between fifty and one hundred books (original and reprint) in the works at any one time, with proofs going from printer to proofreader to author and back to the printer for paging, then back to the author again for indexing. Schedules carefully drawn up for this traffic may be thrown off by delays in printing, failure of an author to return proofs on time, and sudden rush jobs to meet the schedule of a book club. In such an emergency, priorities must be decided by the production manager.

Before the production manager begins shopping around for suppliers for a book, some decisions have to be made. Will printing be by hot type or by computer photocomposition? By letterpress or offset? On a sheet-fed or web-fed press? Will the binding be hard or soft? How big is the print run, and are reprints expected?

Then the production manager goes out to market.

A low-budget book may be given to typesetters and printers with low rates even though they are slow. Speed in the production of an "instant" book may be more important than cost. Quality work may cost both money and delays. Sometimes a book goes to a single manufacturer, who will do the typesetting, printing, and binding.

Cost estimates in a time of inflation are a nightmare, since printers and other suppliers will not commit themselves to a price for more than a few months ahead. Books are sometimes priced only tentatively when they are announced, because the price may have to be raised by the time they are actually published. A realistic schedule for the production of a book after receipt of the author's typescript is one year. Press time and paper may be hard to get. Authors sometimes fail to read and return proofs on time. Two months must be added to the schedule for trade books to permit shipments to bookstores and the sending out of review copies.

Design and production are often combined in the same department. In a small house the production manager may supervise, or even personally do, the design. In a very small house (about a dozen books a year) production and design may be done by free-lancers or by another publishing house, which may also handle marketing. A house with up to one hundred books a year may have a production manager and several assistants, who also handle routine design; special design jobs would be farmed out to free-lancers. The biggest houses may have a staff of fifty in design and production. Publishers of textbooks and children's books use the most designers; after them come trade book publishers, then paperback houses. Manufacturers sometimes have a design department, and there are independent design companies.

Obviously a designer should have some interest in art, and a production worker in business and printing technology. Someone whose prime interest is editing can profit by an entry-level job in design or production to find out how these parts of a publishing house function, but anyone who aspires to advance here must have, or acquire, some special knowledge. In the past a production manager often had worked in typesetting and printing shops, paper mills, and binderies, and had learned about printing by letterpress, lithography, and gravure. Today, production people must improve their knowledge to cover computer photocomposition—and possibly transmission of text by facsimile. The New York executive vacationing in Florida now gets his *Wall Street Journal* on time—a facsimile edition transmitted by satellite.

Colleges and universities are now offering more programs in publishing technology. A student to whom a formal degree program is not locally available might improvise a program in a local college, possibly at night school while getting practical experience on a job. A program for either production or design might include a heavy dose of English, graphic arts, and publishing techniques, plus the sciences used in printing—chemistry, physics, electronics. In the later semesters the designer would concentrate on graphics and the production worker on science and business administration.

Marketing

The marketing manager, like the rest of the department managers, has to cope with the fact that every book is a separate product and requires a separate marketing plan. Like the production manager, the marketing manager is wrapped up in details about all these products—which books are in what stage of manufacture, when they will appear, what features they have that can serve as a hook for advertising, when advertising copy should be sent out. Of course an advertising plan and budget were formulated in the early days of the project, and the manager knows the price and discounts and whether the book will be sold through bookstores, by direct mail, or by other means. These plans are upset if production fails to produce the book on time (a chronic situation).

The method or methods by which any one title is sold depend on the kind of book it is. The selling effort must be concentrated on the person who will decide to buy the book or to recommend it. A general reader is solicited through bookstores and national advertising or direct mail. The approach is different for a school superintendent or the head of a college department. It is different still if the customer is a doctor. A marketing department usually has specialists in each of the various ways of marketing books.

Few American bookstores compare with the great European booksellers. There are over 12,000 book outlets in the United States, but only a handful attempt to stock the most important new hardback and paperback books plus a good selection of older books in print. Small bookstores are often variety stores, handling stationery and gifts as well as books.

Bookstores of any size, especially in population centers, are served by sales representatives. A good sales representative—and bookstores complain that there are too few good ones—is of great help to the bookseller. The sales representative gets to know each bookstore in the territory and the kind of customers it serves, and advises the store on what to buy. Records are kept, and the store is advised when to reorder. Good sales representatives are the advance antennae of the publishing house and can sense how books are being received. Their feedback guides the marketing manager in decisions about stepping up advertising or changing its approach, and is useful to other departments in planning future editions and books.

Publishers support bookstores further by mailings of catalogs and brochures and by advertising in trade papers for booksellers. Large publishing houses have their own sales representatives; smaller houses distribute through the larger houses or employ sales representatives who work on commission for a number of publishers. A large house may have a hundred representatives covering the various regions in the country.

Mass market paperbacks are sold through newsstands and drugstores in addition to bookstores. Most of these outlets are served by wholesalers, but publishers sell directly to supermarkets and store chains like Woolworth's.

Since bookstores are so inadequate in distributing books, they are supplemented by direct marketing. Direct selling, especially to rural customers, is an old tradition—Sears, Roebuck's catalog has long been a national institution, as has the door-to-door book agent with his encyclopedias and Bibles. Advertising books by mail to the customer, and, since the 1920's, through book clubs, has reached a new market far from bookstores.

Book clubs get books at reduced cost by joining the publisher's print run or by printing their own (often cheaper) editions. They pay the publisher a royalty, and offer guarantees as high as $100,000 for the most popular books. Book clubs have increased the number of book readers enormously, if only for selected titles, and they have, no doubt, gotten some readers into the habit of reading for the first time.

Publishers love the book clubs, and in fact all the

outlets that buy subsidiary rights for paperback, foreign, or translated editions—or anything else. Without the sale of subsidiary rights, the publisher might simply break even or lose money on a book. Subsidiary rights are so important that they are sought at early stages of the project—indeed the book may not be published at all if subsidiary rights cannot be sold. Large publishers have several employees in the subsidiary department. Publishers may hold auctions on books with great potential and invite paperback houses to submit bids. Sometimes joint publication by the hardback and paperback publisher is arranged. The subsidiary rights department is another place where a beginner may learn the business.

In 1972 libraries of all kinds bought an estimated $448 million worth of books, or 14 percent of total U.S. consumer sales. Libraries buy a proportionately larger percentage of books published in quantities under five thousand copies, and so make it possible for many such books to be born. About 75 percent of sales to libraries are made through wholesalers and jobbers—a welcome arrangement for the libraries, since they do not have to place thousands of orders directly with publishers, and for the publishers, since they do not have to process all these individual orders.

Since textbooks form so large a part of the book business, any publisher who issues them has very special salespersons, usually former teachers, to approach the buyers. Books for the elementary and high school ("elhi") market are bought mostly by school districts, but in twenty-three states a state board approves selected titles which the districts may buy. The publisher's salespersons make calls on and presentations to school authorities, and distribute free sample copies—perhaps 20,000 copies of a single major book in one year. The salesperson may return (perhaps as stipulated in the contract) to demonstrate to teachers the use of a particular book.

College textbooks are selected by department heads, professors, and instructors, and students buy the textbooks through college bookstores.

Selling technical books to doctors, lawyers, engineers, and so forth, is another specialty. The salesperson is, or becomes, something of an expert in the subject and may make calls on individuals or institutions, or help in writing direct mailings on the books. This employee tells the publisher what is going on in the field and may suggest possible authors or subjects for books. Being a salesperson combines travel, wide contacts with people, and a good salary plus commissions.

Selling in foreign countries has special problems, and most publishers employ foreign sales representatives, usually American companies whose salespersons travel abroad.

The size and cost of an advertising campaign for a book depends on the book and the market. The budget for an important textbook may be very large, including as it does the distribution of so many free copies, but such promotion is tailored to the market and can be expected to pay off. Promotion of scientific books also reaches a select market.

Promotion for trade books for the general public is the biggest gamble and the hardest market to reach. National advertising pays off very poorly. The standard publicity package for trade books is inclusion in the publisher's seasonal and general catalog—the latter also a part of the massive *Publishers Trade Annual;* distribution of two hundred to five hundred review copies; and inclusion in ads for libraries and booksellers in *Publishers Weekly, Library Journal,* and other trade publications. Major books will be advertised in book review media such as the *New*

York Times Book Review and in some important newspapers and magazines. This publicity is intended to support the retail market; and it fails if the book can't be found in bookstores. Some publishers have departments to do all space buying, copywriting and design; some use advertising agencies for all or part of such services.

Getting exposure for books through reviews is difficult. There are only a handful of regular book review media. Other newspapers and magazines carry one or more reviews in each issue. Professional journals do much better, but their reviews often appear a year or more after the book is published. Original paperbacks are finally getting attention from reviewers, although there is still a prejudice against reviewing reprints. Getting exposure for authors on radio and television is even more difficult and takes a lot of effort by the publisher's public relations people, especially for an important network show. A small publisher may have only one public relations person or even one person doing both PR and advertising. A large publisher may have a department of several PR people and secretaries, or a PR person for each line of books.

Accounting

The problems of accounting in publishing are out of all proportion to the size of the business. The accounting manager, like other department managers, must cope with the fact that each book is a separate product, with its own estimates, costs, royalty schedule, marketing plan, price, and discount. Overhead must be allocated among all these separate products. Orders from bookstores often contain inadequate or inaccurate information, and are hard to process. Financial plans and forecasts are difficult to make, because nobody can accurately predict the tastes of readers even a few years ahead, and because changes in government funding may alter the market for textbooks. This department needs clerks, computer operators, bookkeepers, and accountants.

Financial managers—especially those imposed by a conglomerate that has just bought a publishing business—believe in producing items that will have the best sale and make the most money. This is one of the reasons why everybody on the team that produces that unique product, a book, has a say in most decisions. Just as the hard head of the financial manager may temper the literary enthusiasm of the senior editor for a book with too limited appeal, the taste of the senior editor may temper the financial manager's dedication to profit.

Management

Editing, finance, production, and other departments are coordinated by the general manager, who works through the department managers and knows about their contacts with authors, agents, bookstores, printers, banks—and readers. The manager also knows what the competition is doing.

One management problem is attracting and training good employees. Publishers used to have their pick of bright young people because of the prestige and glamour of the business, but there is now a shortage of talented help, particularly in textbook and science publishing, and salaries have gone up.

As Frederic Warburg says, publishing is not a purely rational occupation. It requires energy, enthusiasm, optimism and pessimism, the ability to make decisions, a willingness to guess, all manner of unconscious processes in assessing the popular appeal of a book—and something of the talents of a circus barker in selling it.

QUALIFICATIONS,
EDUCATIONAL AND PERSONAL

Replying to an inquiry about jobs open to someone with a liberal arts education, Doubleday reported 60 to 100 such employees in a variety of jobs. Doubleday publishes about 700 books a year in fiction, nonfiction, natural history, Protestant and Catholic books, and children's books. A degree is preferred, though not required, and Ph.D.'s are welcome. Literature is not necessarily the preferred major. A broad spectrum of minors is helpful, plus foreign languages.

Harper & Row, whose trade division issues about 200 titles in general fiction and nonfiction, has under 100 people working as editorial assistants and assistant editors in the adult trade, paperback, and religious departments, and in various capacities in sales, advertising, and publicity. There, a degree is not necessary except in the textbook division, and the major is irrelevant except in textbooks.

Knopf, with 100 titles, has around 55 such jobs. A degree is not required, but almost everybody has one. There is no preferred major, but employees in its editorial department tend to have backgrounds in literature or history. However, training in science, political science, and economics would be useful. Production and design personnel may have degrees in art.

Popular Library, with over 300 mass market paperback titles annually, has six people as editors and proofreaders, including a production editor, a managing editor, and a copy editor. A Ph.D. degree is considered a hindrance, not a help, and literature is *not* the preferred major.

Mason/Charter, publishing 70 trade and technical books a year, has 25 to 30 employees of this kind. A degree is practically necessary, but a Ph.D. is again a hindrance.

Women have, in the past, often been given entry to publishing because they could be paid less than men. They have dominated the children's book part of the business, although men are now nudging into this specialty. Competition for children's time being what it is, some publishers have reduced or eliminated their juvenile titles.

By 1976 there seemed to be no prejudice against women in the lower echelons of publishing, although the fight for a top job might be tough. Above the routine office level, Doubleday had a ratio of two females to one male and had some female top executives. Harper's was ending discrimination at all levels; it had at least 50 percent women editors in its trade department, a female salesperson, and a female department head; in the reverse direction it had a number of male secretaries and clerical employees. Knopf had a ratio of about fifty-five to forty-five in favor of women, and one woman vice-president. Popular Library made women welcome, and Mason/Charter favored them sixty to forty and had a woman vice-president.

GETTING A JOB

Publishers offer some specific advice about the people they want and how to prepare for and get a job. Stewart Richardson, editor in chief of Doubleday, is looking for creativity, industry, ambition, the ability to get along with people of all sorts—which writers are. He says previous editing or selling shows interest in the job, and recommends the Harvard/ Radcliffe summer course in Publishing Procedures and books about publishing. Doubleday is of course very large, and Richardson suggests you go to the personnel department, but says a good letter to an executive doesn't hurt.

M. S. Wyeth, Jr., editor in chief of Harper's, looks for curiosity and interest in many things; imagination touched with a sense of the practical and the possible; creativity, patience, and tact. Disposition is important; he doesn't want nervous types who can't cope with pressure and can't deal with people. He thinks any practical experience is helpful, the more closely related to the book business the better. He advises: "Learn something about the business by working in a bookstore or wholesaler before coming to a publisher. Try to get a feel of what different publishers publish, what a variety of books are offered and the markets for them. Be willing to start at the bottom and stick with it for a year or two. Show your employer your interest and willingness to do more and learn more by asking questions, volunteering to read manuscripts, etc. Don't expect promotions or changes to come along without seeking them out, but don't be overly impatient. It's a small business and there are many who want into it." To get a job, he says you should try to make personal contacts with people in the company.

Knopf vice-president and senior editor Ashbel Green suggests experience in college journalism and book reviewing. He says: "There is a combination of things I react to: energy, spark, a real interest in books. I look for a person who has done something on his or her own and shows some editorial aptitude, someone who wants to be an editor. A potential editor ought to have a wide range of interests plus one or two specialties." He says very few publishing houses have meaningful personnel departments, and suggests that an applicant write to a senior executive, explaining his interests, and follow up with a phone call for an appointment.

Popular Library's editor in chief Patrick O'Connor suggests a background in selling, editing, or familiarity with the graphic arts and printing. O'Connor doesn't like the average literature majors, who are Henry James scholars in disguise. "They dissemble. They're overeducated and pretentious. Four (sometimes six) years of close textual examination of the novels of Henry James, Edith Wharton, James Joyce, etc., is no qualification for mass market editing. A mass market editor must have a taste for trash and supertrash and must be able to distinguish the rhinestone from the zircon. Half of these little so-and-sos can't."

O'Connor defends the "gothic": "The mass market popular works of fiction are simply nineteenth-century novels of limited insight and uncomplicated characters. They have a noble tradition and are the cornerstone of publishing in the United States. If you can't read a 'nurse' or a 'gothic' novel with some pleasure, you have no business in the paperback field."

O'Connor is looking for passion, attention to detail, and addiction to the printed word: "If, when the conductor hands you back your bus ticket, you read it, and if there is nothing else to read in the house, you read the labels on the medicine bottles, you are on your way." Popular Library editor in chief O'Connor recommends the personal approach in seeking a job.

Mason/Charter's vice-president and managing editor Jane Tonero is looking for neatness, promptness, courtesy, accuracy, intelligence, adaptability, a good attitude, and flexibility. The company will possibly accept a short circuit of the personnel department in applying for a job.

Jane Chavis of the Association of American Publishers believes it takes a combination of energy, curiosity, intelligence, perseverance, and downright love of books to succeed in publishing. The emphasis in all publishing houses seems to be on the enterprising, imaginative self-starter.

Should you take any job to get a toehold in publishing? The consensus seems to be yes. Whether you remain in a dead-end job is up to your own initiative. Not all companies promote from within, but there is usually some flexibility about moving from one department to another if they are related. A job as secretary and assistant to an editor is a real bonanza. A few publishers have a training program, among them Popular Library and the Random House group, to which Knopf belongs. Random House conducts a course for about thirty employees, with weekly lectures and give-and-take among executives in all parts of the company.

Publishing is the communications medium in which there is the least academic interest, and many young people have no access to courses in publishing. If you can get inside the business, you can start asking questions and learning—the judgment and insight of a good editor come only with experience anyway. But you should try to offer something in pertinent skill or experience. Every prospective editor should of course be a good typist and have a good telephone manner, and should be able to handle occasional writing jobs for book jackets and catalogs. A prospective designer might offer a portfolio of drawings, whether published or not, with sketches and specifications for all the sections of one or more books. And a prospective production worker with some experience in computer photocomposition will be very welcome.

If you don't live near a big publishing center, look over the university presses in your area. You can get experience there as well as in a big company, although jobs are few and the pay is poor. Local printers and compositors, including the printing plant of your local newspaper, can provide technical experience. If you are somewhere near a publishing house while you are in school, scrape up acquaintance with somebody on the inside and try to get a summer job. Practice enterprise, for it is a skill you will need in the publishing business.

SALARIES

Publishing has not traditionally been the road to riches, although some publishers have made fortunes. Publishing used to be considered an occupation for "gentlemen"—that is, men with private incomes who could afford to work for prestige rather than for money. Salaries in publishing are still not high compared with other trades. One of the fringe benefits must still be the interest of the job—good editors and book salespeople care about the books they work with.

Editorial secretary-assistants seldom earn as much as secretaries in a business office. In most cases, assistant trade editors, associate editors, and editors make considerably less than officers of comparable status in commercial and industrial firms. Salaries on the administrative and sales side are comparably low.

Production and management jobs pay somewhat better. Staff designers also earn salaries in a medium range. Free-lancers in design are not usually beginners, but more often experienced former staff members. Competition in free-lance design is heavy. Free-lance production work may be done on a cost-plus basis.

SATISFACTIONS OF A CAREER IN PUBLISHING

Book publishing is a happy combination of the creative and the practical. The staff in a publishing house take the ideas and dreams that the author has put down, perhaps in tentative form, work with the author to clarify ideas and shape them up, then put them into the form of that ancient and magic object, a book, to be sold in the marketplace. Without the painstaking work of editors in unearthing and selecting the best books and making them into professional pieces of writing, many fine books would never be born. The power of a free press is demonstrated by the fact that the first thing a dictator does is to take over the broadcasting stations and newspapers, and burn the books.

People in book publishing meet all kinds of interesting types—not only authors but also their kindred workers, who have a variety of skills and background. And, since every book is a new product and a fresh challenge, they don't get bored. They're part of the contemporary scene—and helping to shape the future. And they develop skills that bring them a good income and fairly secure employment.

8

Education: Programs and Courses

Opportunities for education in the various communications arts vary. Courses and programs in journalism and in advertising and public relations are offered widely; courses in radio, film, and television less widely. Book publishing seems to be the most neglected, probably because it is concentrated in New York and there is little call for graduates of publishing programs in other areas.

The Department of Mass Communications of the University of South Florida is described at length as an example of communications education in colleges and universities. The USF program covers advertising, broadcasting, films, magazines, news-editorial journalism, public relations, and visual communication (which includes photojournalism). It does not cover book publishing. The programs at New York University cover writing for film, television, newspapers, and promotion, and the production of film, videotape, and television programs. NYU also has a Center for Publishing and Graphic Design. Pratt Institute and the Modern Media Institute are examples of other types of communications programs.

Education for book publishing and printing technology, offered less widely than other specialties, is stressed here. The program at Rochester Institute of

Technology and the prestigious summer course at Harvard/Radcliffe are covered in detail. And because in many localities the student cannot find a major or minor program in book publishing, but only isolated courses tucked away in schools of journalism or library science, some of these courses are listed, as well as some longer programs for the student who wants to get at least a glimpse of the realm of book publishing.

REPRESENTATIVE PROGRAMS

UNIVERSITY OF SOUTH FLORIDA
4202 E. Fowler Avenue
Tampa, FL 33620

The University of South Florida has more than 23,000 students, faculty, and staff members; over 100 instructional, research, and service programs; and a 65-million-dollar physical plant of 40 major buildings. A little more than half (54 percent) of the students are from the Tampa area. The majority are over age twenty-two. About 14,000 are enrolled part time, and many have jobs. A high proportion are married, with one or both of the couple studying at USF.

The Florida state university system, administered from Tallahassee, now consists of nine public universities. A USF student is normally admitted at the beginning of the junior year as a major to one of the nine colleges. The Department of Mass Communications is one of the most popular. It was started in 1969, and by the end of 1974 had graduated over 500 majors—70 percent of whom report that they are employed in a professional media job. In 1973–74 the department had over a thousand majors, and the number was reduced through tighter entrance requirements and a stiffer program. The department now requires three quarters of freshman English or a waiver thereof plus two courses, "Writing for the Mass Media" and "Mass Media and Society," as prerequisites for the major—plus a typing speed of 30 words per minute. Prejournalism majors are also encouraged to take introductory courses in logic; issues in American civilization; semantics; computer science; economic problems; crime and society; national, state, and local government; and United States history.

Within the communications major the student chooses a "sequence"—Advertising, Broadcasting, Film, Magazines, News-Editorial Journalism, Public Relations, or Visual Communication (including photojournalism). Each sequence requires twenty hours of specialized courses, plus twenty hours of related courses.

The philosophy of the department is that training in mass communications must be based on a sound liberal arts education. Mass Communications is an undergraduate program, with some senior courses spilling over into the graduate school. Of the total 180 hours of the program, only forty-eight may be taken in Mass Communications; the rest are in liberal arts. The department has plans for a master's degree program, and in 1976 applied for accreditation with the American Council for Education in Journalism.

The curriculum introduces students to the theories, principles, and problems of communications, and emphasizes the concept of freedom of information as essential in a democracy. Students are prepared for leadership and creative work, as well as for the routine processing of information. They must be able to generate the ideas they process, and to understand the structure and functions of mass media systems as well as the basic processes of communication.

Faculty members have all had practical experience in the subjects they teach and bring the realities of the working world to the classroom.

The Tampa area has six major daily newspapers, six television stations, more than two dozen radio stations, many public relations and advertising agencies, and printing and publishing companies. Personnel from these establishments often speak to classes and seminars, and some have served as "teaching adjuncts."

The department uses the latest and most modern equipment in its classrooms and laboratories. In the Reporting Laboratory each student has a desk with a built-in Selectric typewriter and a telephone. An elaborate pushbutton system permits students to practice interviewing each other by phone. Audiovisual aids include all up-to-date equipment from movie projectors to closed-circuit television. In the nearby Instructional Materials Center, students may view videotapes on individual small television sets. For example, presentations of prominent guest lecturers are taped and stored. Students may simply pick up the phone in their dormitory rooms or apartments, dial the IMC, and ask that the tape be played to them over the phone.

In the News Editing Laboratory next to the Reporting Laboratory, students work at copy desks with the day's news from the United Press International "A" wire. The room is equipped for audiovisual presentations. The department plans to get at least one video display terminal to use in the news-editing class, and hopes to wire it to the computer in the Typography Lab so that students can edit copy from the UPI wire, transmit it to the computers, and then see their finished product.

The Photography Laboratory has four individual

darkrooms, including one for color processing, a large developing room with 10 enlargers, and a room for processing film. Students may check out Pentax 35mm or Rolleiflex cameras, light meters, and strobe units.

The Typography Laboratory contains light tables, perforators, three Compugraphic computers including a Headliner, and equipment for making and processing film. A beginning journalism student learns how to operate these machines—not to become a keypunch operator or a printer, but to become familiar with the processes. The student punches out a reporter's article on an "idiot tape" to be fed into a computer, which will spew out another tape with justified copy. The new tape is fed into a second computer for computer photocomposition. Letters are automatically arranged and printed on film ready for pasting up on a page dummy. A similar machine sets headline "type." When the film is all pasted up, it too is photographed, and a full-sized sheet of film is produced for a plate for an offset press. At night the laboratory is used to process the student daily newspaper, including ad makeup and full-page layouts.

Students in Magazine Article Writing study content and types of magazines, query letters, trends, the market situation. Then they write—and rewrite —and must send off an article to some magazine they have studied thoroughly. Many of their articles are published. Students in the film classes work together as teams to write, produce, and film their own productions in 16mm or 35mm film. The department owns a good deal of cinematography equipment.

In their senior year, the best students are invited to enroll in special "practicums," in which they work one full day or night a week with a downtown public relations firm, advertising agency, magazine, or newspaper, under the supervision of a professional. In the Reporting Practicum, for example, a student assigned to one of the six or seven area daily newspapers usually goes along with a veteran reporter on a beat, then is assigned to do stories on his or her own. The student gets by-lines as a "staff writer" or "staff correspondent." Attending meetings of city councils, police courts, school board meetings, and so on, and meeting city officials and record keepers, the young reporter then writes investigative and analytical articles.

One difficulty with this fieldwork is that MassCom students, whether native to the area or not, develop ties with the local media employers and want to continue this cozy relationship after graduation. Since it is neither possible nor desirable that all local talent should be so inbred, students must broaden their view and be willing to relocate, even to a bad climate, to get a job.

Many students work for the award-winning student daily newspaper, *The Oracle*—an impressive product of up to thirty-six pages an issue, with professional-quality photos and a gratifying supply of ads. With a budget approaching $200,000 a year, it is 80 percent self-supporting. It covers general and local as well as campus news, and leases two UPI wire service teleprinters to cover the national and international news for its campus readers. It has newsstand racks in area supermarkets and major stores. The publication is now separated from the department, and is independent; its student staff determines its news and editorial content.

The typical MassCom student is serious-minded. A student's interest may center on one of the student chapters of professional media organizations such as Visage, the photojournalism group; Sigma Delta Chi, the journalist group; or the Public Relations Society of America. Students may also join political or special interest groups. Many have part-time jobs.

In recent years the pendulum in education has swung toward "relevancy" in the selection of majors and electives. Students prefer a major that will get them a job—accounting, journalism, engineering. Fewer and fewer students select modern languages, philosophy, English, history, the arts. The journalism student will more likely take an elective in urban government than in Milton—he can "use" the course in government. However, MassCom students at USF do choose a rich variety of electives.

At USF, students from small high schools soon cease to feel lost. Each sequence in MassCom has 100 to 150 students and classes may number from fifteen to eighteen—a small group indeed. All classes, from freshman-level on up, are taught by experienced professors, not by student teaching assistants.

USF also offers a major in the Theater Arts Department. Students may lay a foundation for a professional career in the theater or continue their studies at the graduate level. In addition, students from other departments and colleges may participate in the studies and work of the department. Theater Arts majors concentrate in either performance or design and technology. Mass Communications majors who concentrate on films or television have an opportunity to observe the related techniques of the theater.

NEW YORK UNIVERSITY
100 Washington Square East
New York, NY 10003

New York University has more than 30,000 students in degree-conferring divisions. It also offers many courses outside the degree programs which may earn Continuing Education Units (CEUs) or credit toward a certificate. The courses noted here are in the School of Continuing Education.

NYU offers courses in writing and marketing fiction and nonfiction, and in writing for film, television, newspapers, and promotion. There is also a program in Film, Videotape, and Television Production, taught by industry professionals. Workshop classes use fully equipped facilities. A Certificate in Film is awarded to students who complete four required courses—The Film Medium, Film Production I and II, Film Editing Workshop—plus at least one elective.

The Center for Publishing and Graphic Design was established in 1936 for adults. Students can qualify for a Certificate of Achievement. Courses in book publishing include Media in America, Book Production Workshop, Advanced Book Design, Children's Book Publishing, Proofreading and Copy-editing, Book Editing Workshop, Marketing Trade Books, and Direct Marketing. There are two courses in magazine publishing. Courses in graphics and printing include Introduction to the Graphic Arts, Design, Book Illustration, and Printing Reproduction Processes and Materials.

THE HARVARD SUMMER SCHOOL / RADCLIFFE
   COURSE IN PUBLISHING PROCEDURES
10 Garden Street
Cambridge, MA 02138

This course has been called the shortest graduate school in the world. It was started over twenty-five years ago as a pioneer course in the subject, and its 1,400 graduates (enrollment has always been limited and is now 75 a year) have thoroughly infiltrated the industry, some in top jobs. At the end of a session

118

there are almost always more jobs offered to graduates than there are students. The six-week course for recent college graduates operates on the principle of overkill, and inundates the student with information and exposure to publishing establishments and personnel.

The course is directed by Mrs. Diggory Venn, who recruits and screens students (four times as many apply as can be admitted), goes after lecturers and drags them away from their offices or ivory towers for a day, plans the work, and places students in jobs.

The course is intended to convey an understanding of the requirements and opportunities of publishing; to provide basic training in publishing skills; and to bring students into direct contact with publishers. Practical instruction is provided by more than fifty important book and magazine executives. The program mixes lectures, seminars, workshops, and field trips. As far as possible, students perform the actual functions of publishing. Half the time is given to book publishing and half to magazine publishing. Two special workshops take up book design and production, and magazines. In the latter, student groups prepare their own forty-eight-page magazines. Field trips cover publishing houses, compositors and printers, suppliers, and wholesalers.

The course covers such topics as creative editing, copy-editing/proofreading, picture research, the economics of publishing, selling books by direct mail, the bookstore, university presses, children's books, educational publishing, international publishing, multimedia publishing, subsidiary rights, advertising/promotion, authors and editors, printing and production, and magazine development.

Students learn that publishing entails a lot of hard work and a commitment to the job. One student, daughter of a publisher, said she believed the course acted as a sort of decompression chamber between the academic world and the real world of publishing. The decompression may be too swift for some students and they may get the bends. Because of the competition, students must apply early and arrange an interview.

PUBLISHING INSTITUTE.
GRADUATE SCHOOL OF LIBRARIANSHIP
University of Denver, CO 80210

The Publishing Institute offers a concentrated four-week summer course which combines practical workshops in editing and marketing with lecture and teaching sessions conducted by experts from all areas of publishing. The university also offers various courses for librarians and others on the book business, including short courses of one or two weeks in December.

ROCHESTER INSTITUTE OF TECHNOLOGY
One Lomb Memorial Drive
Rochester, NY 14623

The Rochester Institute of Technology trains professional and technical workers to meet the needs of Rochester's high-skill industries. It offers its more than 7,000 day students subjects that are taught seldom or not at all in other institutions. RIT's College of Graphic Arts and Photography, including the School of Photographic Arts and Sciences, the School of Printing, and the Graphic Arts Research Center, offers programs leading to a B.S. in Photographic Science and Instrumentation, a B.S. in Professional Photography, and a B.F.A. in Photographic Illustration. Other degree programs are in Photographic Management and Marketing, Biomedical Photography, and Biomedical Photographic Communications. There are M.S. programs in photography.

The School of Printing offers programs leading to a B.S. in printing, with fourteen options for specialization. There are M.S. programs in Printing Technology and Printing Education.

The Graphic Arts Research Center, with its own full-time staff, also conducts short special courses for professionals in this field. There is feedback between the college and the graphic industry in Rochester, a world center of graphic arts.

Photography students are offered two courses in filmmaking, from scriptwriting to sound editing. The curriculum in photographic management prepares students for management positions in the photographic processing and finishing industry. The curriculum in biomedical photographic communications covers the advanced techniques of media production used in medicine and research, with electives in filmmaking, television, and printing. A student can qualify as a Registered Biological Photographer.

The School of Printing is the largest degree-granting school in its field in the country. Emphasis is on careers in printing technology, printing production, and printing management. Students are given an appreciation of the aesthetic qualities of good printing and an understanding of the applications of science and engineering in the graphic arts. Some course sequences include: Book Design and Book Production; Design and Typography; Composing Room Procedures; Lithographic Technology; Packaging Printing; Reproduction Photography; Estimating; Computer Applications; Newspaper Production Management; Financial Management; Personnel Management; Production Management; Sales and Marketing.

121

The printing industry employs not only printing specialists but also chemists, physicists, engineers, accountants, marketing specialists, designers, copy editors, computer specialists, production and traffic managers, and packaging specialists. Students can elect to study any of these subjects in RIT's nine colleges and combine them with study of the printing business itself.

PRATT INSTITUTE
Brooklyn, NY 11205

Pratt has about 4,500 students, in Schools of Architecture, Art and Design, Engineering (undergraduate only), Liberal Arts and Sciences, and Library and Information Science (graduate only).

The School of Art and Design has expanded and developed. Designers have gone beyond the category of commercial artists; they provide entertainment, transmit information, and create efficient and satisfying environments for human use. A new performing arts program offers majors in dance and theater arts. The Graphics Center at 831 Broadway, Manhattan, functions as a proving ground for qualified artists, art teachers, graduate art students, and printmakers who want to study advanced etching, engraving, relief printing, and mixed media under expert printmakers.

Formal programs in the School of Art and Design are Communications Art; Communications Design; Graphic Arts and Illustration; Dance; Environmental Design; Fashion Design; Film; History of Art; Industrial Design; Merchandising and Fashion Management; Painting and Drawing; Photography; Printmaking; Sculpture and Ceramics; Theater Arts.

The Communications Design program is concerned with creating visual concepts through the mass media of print, television, and film. Courses in advertising, graphic design, illustration, and packaging are supplemented by offerings in typography, film, photography, printmaking, drawing, painting, technical courses, and so on. Emphasis is on agency and studio procedures. Graduates are prepared for careers in advertising, graphic design, illustration, and exhibition and packaging design.

MODERN MEDIA INSTITUTE
556 Central Avenue
St. Petersburg, FL 33701

The Modern Media Institute was created in 1975 to offer high school and college students and media professionals opportunities for study and learning unavilable elsewhere. Although MMI gives no academic credit or degrees, students interested in earning credit toward graduation for work done at MMI can expect to present a respectable case for credit to their institutions. Eckerd College in St. Petersburg gives such credit. The summer program is designed for university students. At present it covers Design and Illustration, Photographic Reporting, News Writing in Four Weeks, Broadcast News Production, Critical Writing, and Creative Feature Writing. Courses planned for the future include Public Affairs Reporting, Investigative Reporting, Social Science Methods of Newsmen, Creative Editing, Media Management, Modern Production Methods. MMI also works with high school students and offers a program for high school newspaper editors and advertising/ business managers. Local high school editors can prepare camera-ready copy for their newspapers in MMI's laboratory. Many tuition fellowships are available. Other facets of the mass media—graphics, broadcasting, and film—will be added later.

ACCREDITED PROGRAMS IN COMMUNICATIONS

The American Council on Education for Journalism, representing both educational and professional media organizations, is the formally recognized agency for the accreditation of programs for professional education in journalism and mass communications in institutions of higher learning in the United States. The name and address of the institution accredited, and the programs accredited, are listed here.

Arizona, University of: Tucson, AZ 85721—Department of Journalism (News-Editorial)

Arizona State University: Tempe, AZ 85281—Department of Journalism (News-Editorial)

Boston University: Boston, MA 02215—School of Public Communications (News-Editorial, Public Relations)

California, University of: Berkeley, CA 94720—School of Journalism (News-Editorial—Graduate Program)

California State University: Fresno, CA 93740—Department of Journalism (News-Editorial)

California State University: Fullerton, CA 92631—Department of Communications (News-Editorial)

California State University: Northridge, CA 91324—Department of Journalism (News-Editorial)

California State University: San Jose, CA 95192—Department of Journalism and Advertising (Advertising, Reporting and Editing)

Southern California, University of: University Park, Los Angeles, CA 90007—School of Journalism (News-Editorial, Public Relations)

Colorado, University of: Boulder, CO 80302—School of Journalism (Advertising, News-Editorial)

Colorado State University: Fort Collins, CO 80523—Department of Technical Journalism (Technical-Industrial, Radio-Television, News and Documentaries)

Columbia University: New York, NY 10027—Graduate School of Journalism (News-Editorial—Graduate Program)

Drake University: Des Moines, IA 50311—School of Journalism (News-Editorial, Advertising)

Florida, University of: Gainesville, FL 32601—College of Journalism and Communications (Advertising, Editorial-News, Radio and Television—general)

Georgia, University of: Athens, GA 30602—Henry W. Grady School of Journalism (Advertising, Public Relations, Radio-Television-Film, News-Editorial)

Houston, University of: Houston, TX 77004—Department of Communications (Radio and Television—general)

Illinois, University of: Urbana, IL 61801—College of Communications (Advertising, News-Editorial, Radio-Television)

Northern Illinois University: DeKalb, IL 60115—Department of Journalism (News-Editorial)

Southern Illinois University: Carbondale, IL 62901—Department of Journalism (Advertising, News-Editorial)

Southern Illinois University: Edwardsville, IL 62026—Department of Mass Communications (Television-Radio—general)

Indiana University: Bloomington, IN 47401—School of Journalism (News-Editorial); Department of Telecommunications (Radio-Television—general)

Iowa State University of Science and Technology: Ames, IA 50010—Department of Journalism and Mass Communications (News-Editorial)

Kansas, University of: Lawrence, KS 66045—William Allen White School of Journalism (Advertising, News-Editorial, Radio-Television—general)

Kansas State University: Manhattan, KS 66506—Department of Journalism and Mass Communications (News-Editorial)

Kent State University: Kent, OH 44242—School of Journalism (News-Editorial)

Louisiana State University and Agricultural and Mechanical College: University Station, Baton Rouge, LA 70803—School of Journalism (News-Editorial)

Maryland, University of: College Park, MD 20742—College, of Journalism (News-Editorial, Public Relations)

Memphis State University: Memphis, TN 38152—Department of Journalism (News-Editorial)

Michigan, University of: Ann Arbor, MI 48104—Department of Journalism (News-Editorial—Graduate Program)

Michigan State University: East Lansing, MI 48823—School of Journalism (News-Editorial); Department of Advertising (Advertising)

Minnesota, University of: Minneapolis, MN 55455—School of Journalism and Mass Communications (Advertising, News-Editorial)

Mississippi, University of: University, MS 38677—Department of Journalism (News-Editorial)

Missouri, University of: Columbia, MO 65201—School of Journalism (Advertising, Magazine, News-Editorial, Newspaper Publishing, Photojournalism, Radio-Television News)

Montana, University of: Missoula, MT 59801—School of Journalism (News-Editorial, Radio-Television—general)

Nebraska, University of: Lincoln, NB 68508—School of Journalism (News-Editorial, Advertising, Radio-Television—general)

Nevada, University of: Reno, NV 89507—Department of Journalism (News-Editorial)

New Mexico, University of: Albuquerque, NM 87131—Department of Journalism (News-Editorial)

New York University: New York, NY 10003—Department of Journalism and Mass Communications (News-Editorial)

North Carolina, University of: Chapel Hill, NC 27514—School of Journalism (News-Editorial)

North Dakota, University of: Grand Forks, ND 58201—Department of Journalism (News-Editorial)

Northwestern University: Evanston, IL 60201—Medill School of Journalism (Advertising, News-Editorial, Radio-Television News, Magazine—Graduate Programs)

Ohio State University: Columbus, OH 43210—School of Journalism (News-Editorial, Public Relations, Radio-Television News)

Ohio University: Athens, OH 45701—School of Journalism (Advertising-Management, News-Editorial, Public Relations, Radio-Television News)

Oklahoma, University of: Norman OK 73069—H. H. Herbert School of Journalism (Professional Writing, Public Relations, Advertising, News Communication)

Oklahoma State University: Stillwater, OK 74074—School of Journalism and Broadcasting (Advertising-Management, News-Editorial)

Oregon, University of: Eugene, OR 97403—School of Journalism (Advertising, News-Editorial, Public Relations, Radio-Television News)

Pennsylvania State University: University Park, PA 16802—School of Journalism (Advertising, News-Editorial, Broadcast News)

San Diego State University: San Diego, CA 92182—Department of Journalism (News-Editorial)

South Carolina, University of: Columbia, SC 29208—College of Journalism (News-Editorial, Advertising, Radio-Television)

South Dakota State University: Brookings, SD 57006—Department of Journalism and Mass Communications (News-Editorial)

Syracuse University: Syracuse, NY 13210—S. I. Newhouse School of Public Communications (Advertising, Magazine, News-Editorial, Photojournalism)

Temple University: Philadelphia, PA 19122—Department of Journalism (News-Editorial)

Tennessee, University of: Knoxville, TN 37916—College of Communications (Advertising, News-Editorial)

Texas, University of: Austin, TX 78712—School of Communications (Advertising, Magazine, News-Editorial, Public Relations)

North Texas State University: Denton, TX 76203—Department of Journalism (News-Editorial)

Texas A & M University: College Station, TX 77843—Department of Journalism (News-Editorial, Agricultural Journalism)

Texas Christian University: Fort Worth, TX 76129—Department of Journalism (News-Editorial)

Texas Tech University: Lubbock, TX 79409—Department of Mass Communications (News-Editorial, Advertising, Telecommunications)

Utah, University of: Salt Lake City, UT 84112—Department of Journalism (News-Editorial, Broadcast Journalism, Telecommunications)

Washington, University of: Seattle, WA 98195—School of Communications (News-Editorial, General Radio and Television)

Washington and Lee University: Lexington, VA 24450—Lee Memorial Journalism Foundation (News-Editorial)

West Virginia University: Morgantown, WV 26506—School of Journalism (Broadcasting)

Wisconsin, University of: Madison, WI 53706—School of Journalism and Mass Communications (News-Editorial, Public Relations, Radio-Television News); Department of Agricultural Journalism (Agricultural, Home Economics)

Wisconsin, University of: Milwaukee, WI 53201—Department of Mass Communications (Radio-Television—general)

Accreditation is pending in some new departments. For current information, write to: Executive Secretary, Association for Education in Journalism, 118 Reavis Hall, Northern Illinois University, DeKalb, IL 60115.

ACEJ does not accredit programs leading to a Ph.D., which is considered a research, not a professional, degree.

EDUCATION FOR BROADCASTING

For a list of schools and colleges offering substantial course work in radio and television, a list of junior and community colleges offering a two-year course in broadcasting, and a list of scholarships available to students in radio, write to:

Executive Secretary
Broadcast Education Association
National Association of Broadcasters
1771 N Street, NW
Washington, DC 20036

COURSES IN BOOK PUBLISHING

ARKANSAS

Arkansas State University
College of Communications
State University, AR 72467

ASU offers some 13 undergraduate courses in the graphic arts and printing technology.

CALIFORNIA

University of California, Davis
U.C.D. Extension
Davis, CA 95616

"Of Making Many Books . . ." (X401.1). Undergraduate. Introduction to book development and publication.

University of Southern California
School of Library Science
University Park
Los Angeles, CA 90007

Publications Design and Technology (JOUR475). Undergraduate. Survey of graphic elements in design, production methods, processes, and equipment.

Stanford University
Alumni Association Continuing Education
Stanford, CA 94305

From Manuscript to Magnum Opus. Undergraduate. Introduction to book publishing including case studies of book processing and publishing mechanics.

CANADA

University of British Columbia
School of Librarianship
2075 Westbrook Place
Vancouver, B.C., Canada V6T1WS

Publishing and the Book Trade (L530). Graduate. Introduction to economic, legal, and cultural factors in creating, producing, and marketing books.

University of Toronto
Faculty of Library Science
140 St. George Street
Toronto, Ont., Canada M5S1A6

Contemporary Publishing (2140x). Graduate. Survey of publishing practice from manuscript selection and editing through production and distribution.

CONNECTICUT

University of Connecticut
Department of English
Storrs, CT 06268

Realities of Publishing (ENG217–06). Undergraduate, graduate. Lecture/discussion survey including editing, printing, lexicography, censorship, copyright, subsidiary rights, marketing, bookselling.

DISTRICT OF COLUMBIA

The George Washington University
2130 H Street, NW
Library Suite 621
Washington, DC 20006

Editing, Publications, and Graphic Communications (G-10). Noncredit 12-month certificate course 6 hours per week, designed to give college graduates marketable skills in writing, copy-editing, production, and design.

Editing and Publications Program. Undergraduate, graduate noncredit 42-week certificate program six evening hours per week, to give persons with liberal arts education basic training for jobs in editing and production.

Graduate School of the U.S. Department of Agriculture
Evening Program, Communications and Language Arts
Room 1030, South Building
14th Street and Independence Avenue, SW
Washington, DC 20250

Editing Technical Manuscripts (E2412). *Advanced Practice in Editing* (E2412). Literary and statistical editing, graphics integration. *Intermediate Editing* (E2239). Stresses effectiveness, readability, structure of manuscripts, and techniques of editor aid to authors. *Printing, Layout, and Design* (E2237). *Production and Management of Graphics* (E2181). *Principles of Editing and Their Application* (E2225). *Seminar in Editing* (E2424).

FLORIDA

Florida State University
School of Library Science
Tallahassee, FL 32306

Publishers and Publishing in the United States (LIS580). Graduate. The role and functions of book and other publishing in social, educational, economic, and literary history.

GEORGIA

Atlanta University
School of Library Service
Atlanta, GA 30314

Publishers and Publishing (541). Graduate. Survey of technological innovations affecting twentieth-century

132

book production. Also covers editorial functions, distribution, advertising, and sales.

ILLINOIS

The University of Chicago
University of Chicago Extension
1307 East 60th Street
Chicago, IL 60637

Introduction to Publishing (NW774). Graduate noncredit. Survey, including processes of publishing and economic and social contexts.

Production for Publishers (NW770). Graduate noncredit. Detailed survey of book production from manuscript to bound book supplemented by field trips.

Manuscript Editing (NW771). Graduate noncredit.

The University of Chicago
Graduate Library School
1100 East 57th Street
Chicago, IL 60637

20th-Century Publishing (GLS347). A survey of the publishing industry, manuscript selection, processing, and distribution.

University of Illinois
College of Communications
119 Gregory Hall
Urbana, IL 61801

Journalism II (J360). Undergraduate, graduate. Survey of visual communications with emphasis on developing skills.

Publication Design and Production (233). Undergraduate, graduate. Advanced course in graphic design and printing production.

Typography (204). Undergraduate, graduate. Survey of type lore, dimension and composition methods, platemaking and printing, production economics.

University of Illinois
Graduate School of Library Science
329 Library
Urbana, IL 61801

Typographic Disciplines of the Book (LS310). Undergraduate, graduate. Study of the book as a manufactured object from the Renaissance to the present.

Contemporary Book Publishing (LS443). Graduate. Survey of economic, social, and literary context of publishing with emphasis on author-publisher relations, promotion, distribution, and influence on librarianship.

Southern Illinois University
Department of Journalism
Carbondale, IL 62901

Graphic Communication (J315–3). Undergraduate. History of printing and typography including reproduction processes, technology, selection of graphics, and production techniques.

KANSAS

University Press of Kansas
Journalism School
366 Watson Library
Lawrence, KS 66045

Book Publishing (JOUR504). Undergraduate. Lecture course surveying the entire field including author-publisher relations and careers in book publishing. Emphasis is on structure and operation.

KENTUCKY

University of Kentucky
Department of Art
Lexington, KY 40506

Basics of Graphic Art. Undergraduate. Basic vocational experience in typography and printing.

MASSACHUSETTS

The Bookbuilders of Boston
P.O. Box 717
Boston, MA 02102

Bookbuilders of Boston Workshop. Annual workshop series, information about all facets of the book industry. Weekly September/October meetings plus five field trips explore marketing, advertising, production, materials, composition, graphics, editorial acquisitions, and manuscript-editing.

Simmons College
Department of Communications
300 The Fenway
Boston, MA 02115

Modern Publishing and Librarianship (LS420). Undergraduate. A survey of book publishing—book production, specialized publishing, marketing, international and legal aspects of publishing, and organizations in the industry. Lectures, field trips, individual research papers.

MICHIGAN

Western Michigan University
College of Applied Sciences
Department of Industrial Education
Kalamazoo, MI 49001

Printing Management Curriculum. Undergraduate four-year degree program of 122 credit hours. Combines training in graphic arts, business, industrial supervision, paper science, and general education.

NEW MEXICO

University of New Mexico Press
Albuquerque, NM 87131

History of the Book (ART494, SEC 3, or ENG488, SEC 1). Undergraduate, graduate. A review of 500 years of book-making, printing, and technology. Course stresses examination of actual examples, hands-on typesetting and press experience, and completion of a paper or graphic project.

NEW YORK

State University of New York at Albany
School of Library and Information Science
1400 Washington Avenue
Albany, NY 12222

Publishing in the United States. Graduate. Survey of publishers in American society, including acquisition of manuscripts and production and distribution of books.

Problems in Contemporary Publishing (LIB654). Graduate. Survey of the processes of selecting, producing, and distributing books in the United States and the economic and legal aspects of publishing.

State University of New York
School of Library and Information Sciences
Geneseo, NY 14454

Out-of-Print Book Trade (LIB608). Graduate. Study of the out-of-print book trade and its use in building library collections.

Columbia University
School of Library Service
516 Butler Library
New York, NY 10027

Modern Book Publishing (LSK8373X). Graduate. Survey of contemporary U.S. book publishing practices with some consideration of foreign publishers.

Herbert Lehman College
English Department
Bedford Park Boulevard, West
Bronx, NY 10468

Introduction to Book Publishing (ENG376). Undergraduate. Survey of book publishing from writers' ideas to distributors' procedures. Practical assignments in writing, editing, proofreading.

Hofstra University
English Department
Hempstead, NY 11550

The Theory and Practice of Publishing. Undergraduate, graduate. Introduction to the publishing process from submission of manuscript to publication.

Hunter College of the City University of New York
Center for Lifelong Learning
School of General Studies
Room 241, 695 Park Avenue
New York, NY 10021

Fundamentals of Book Editing, Copy-editing, and Proofreading (e05 526). Noncredit.

Printing Industries of Metropolitan New York, Inc.
The Evening School
461 Eighth Avenue
New York, NY 10001

Certificate courses for employees of the industry:

Graphics and Typographics. Seminar/workshop including application of design in advertising, promotion, and packaging.

Advanced Graphics and Typographics. Invitational seminar/workshop in actual design problems from trademark to packaging.

Elements of Offset Lithography. Lecture/demonstration course in fundamentals of lithographic offset processes. Not an experience in shop training or mechanical operations.

Fundamentals of Production. Practical course suited to production trainees and oriented to commercial printing work. *Proofreading and Copy-editing. Advanced Proofreading and Copy-Editing. Introduction to Printing and*

Printing Processes. Elementary course in factual and visual knowledge of the printing industry. No training in shop practices or mechanical operations.

NORTH CAROLINA

University of North Carolina
School of Library Science
Chapel Hill, NC 27514

Contemporary Publishing and the Book Industry (LS107). Undergraduate, graduate. A survey of present techniques and problems in the production and distribution of communication materials.

OHIO

Kent State University
Department of English
Kent, OH 44242

Editing for Publishers (ENG48020). Undergraduate, graduate. Practical introduction to copy-editing for publishing houses with emphasis on setting copy into type.

Kent State University
School of Journalism
Kent, OH 44242

Introduction to Graphic Communications (K23001). Undergraduate. Graphic expression on paper, cloth, metal, plastic, glass, etc.

OKLAHOMA

University of Tulsa
Faculty of Letters Program in Rhetoric and Writing
Tulsa, OK 74104

Workshop in Editing and Publishing. Undergraduate, graduate. A survey of basic procedures from manuscript development and acquisition to distribution and promotion. Course culminates in completion of a practical group project.

OREGON

Oregon State University
Department of Journalism
Corvallis, OR 97331

Mechanics of Publishing (J335). Undergraduate. Introduction to type and type selection, paper, ink, printing layout, design, and processing.

PENNSYLVANIA

Graphic Arts Education Center
1900 Cherry Street
Philadelphia, PA 19103

Printing Management Program. Undergraduate, graduate. The Graphic Arts Association of Delaware Valley, Inc., through its Graphic Arts Education Center, offers 22 courses in printing management on three campuses: 21 courses at GAADV headquarters in Philadelphia, nine courses at Franklin and Marshall College in Lancaster, and six courses at Lehigh University in Bethlehem. Some new courses are *Metrics for the Graphic Arts, Graphic Arts Billing Procedures, How to Buy Printing,* and *Paper and Papermaking.*

University of Pittsburgh
School of Library and Information Sciences
Pittsburgh, PA 15260

Contemporary Book Production (LS213). Graduate. Skills, techniques, and technologies applied in converting a manuscript into a bound book.

TENNESSEE

University of Tennessee
Graduate School of Library and Information Science
804 Volunteer Boulevard
Knoxville, TN 37916

Contemporary Publishing (LIS5530). Graduate. An introduction to the book publishing process from manuscript through distribution, including economics and promotion.

TEXAS

Texas Woman's University
School of Library Science
Denton, TX 76204

Printing, Publishing, and Book Distribution (LS6503). Offered every other year. Structure, economic characteristics, trends, and technology of publishing.

VIRGINIA

Printing Industries of America, Inc.
1730 North Lynn Street
Arlington, VA 22209

Development Center Workshop/Seminars. An annual series of management awareness programs for operating executives in the printing industry. Preannounced programs, scheduled at hotels across the United States, are guided by industry experts.

Executive Development Program. A ten-day course for executives and managers in graphic arts industries. First and second (senior) year programs, conducted by industry experts, provide lectures, case analyses, and seminars in sales, marketing, production, manufacturing, financial and manpower management, planning, and organization.

The College of William and Mary
Williamsburg, VA 23185

Ferguson Seminar in Publishing. A two-day program offered biannually for students of Virginia colleges. Lectures and classes conducted by active publishing personnel.

WEST VIRGINIA

West Virginia University
School of Journalism

101 Martin Hall
Morgantown, WV 26506

Typography and Printing Processes (JOUR110). Undergraduate. Fundamentals of print production including design and composition.

Bibliography

Adelstein, Michael E., and Pival, Jean G., *The Writing Commitment*. Harcourt Brace Jovanovich, Inc., 1976.

American Association of Advertising Agencies, *Advertising—The Advertising Business and Its Career Opportunities*. Booklet, available free from AAAA, 200 Park Avenue, New York, NY 10017.

Bailey, Herbert S., Jr., *The Art and Science of Book Publishing*. Harper & Row, Publishers, Inc., 1970.

Barzun, Jacques, *Simple and Direct: A Rhetoric for Writers*. Harper & Row, Publishers, Inc., 1975.

———, and Graff, Henry F., *The Modern Researcher*. Rev. ed. Harcourt Brace Jovanovich, Inc., 1970.

Bernstein, Theodore M., *The Careful Writer*. Atheneum Publishers, 1965.

———, *Miss Thistlebottom's Hobgoblins*. Farrar, Straus & Giroux, Inc., 1971.

Bliss, Edward, Jr., and Patterson, John M., *Writing News for Broadcast*. Columbia University Press, 1971.

Cherry, Colin, *On Human Communication*. John Wiley & Sons, Inc., 1957.

Coleman, Ken, *So You Want to Be a Sportscaster*. Hawthorn Books, Inc., 1973.

Dary, David, *Television News Handbook*. Tab Books, 1971.

Dessauer, John P., *Book Publishing: What It Is, What It Does*. R. R. Bowker Company, 1974.

Eastman, Ann Heidbreder, and Lee, Grant, *Education for*

Publishing, A Survey Report. University of Pittsburgh Graduate School of Library and Information Sciences, 1976.

Editor and Publisher, 850 Third Avenue, New York, NY 10022. Weekly.

Exman, Eugene, *The House of Harper: One Hundred and Fifty Years of Publishing.* Harper & Row, Publishers, Inc., 1967.

Fowler, H. W., *A Dictionary of Modern English Usage,* 2d ed. rev. by Sir Ernest Gowers. Oxford University Press, 1965.

Grannis, Chandler B. (ed.), *The Heritage of the Graphic Arts.* R. R. Bowker Company, 1972.

———— (ed.), *What Happens in Book Publishing,* 2d ed. Columbia University Press, 1967.

Gross, Gerald (ed.), *Editors on Editing.* Grosset & Dunlap, Inc., 1962.

Hayakawa, S. I., *Language in Thought and Action.* 3d ed. Harcourt Brace Jovanovich, Inc., 1972.

Hicks, T. G., *Writing for Engineering and Science.* McGraw-Hill Book Co., Inc., 1961.

Hohenberg, John, *The Professional Journalist: A Guide to the Principles and Practices of the News Media,* 3d ed. Holt, Rinehart & Winston, Inc., 1973.

Jackson, Gregory, *Getting Into Broadcast Journalism.* Hawthorn Books, Inc., 1975.

Jovanovich, William, *Now, Barabbas.* Harper & Row, Publishers, Inc., 1964.

Kleppner, Otto S., and Greyser, Stephen, *Advertising Procedure,* 6th ed. Prentice-Hall, Inc., 1973.

Kujoth, Jean Spencer, *Book Publishing: Inside Views.* Scarecrow Press, Inc., 1971.

Landau, Robert M. (ed.), *Proceedings of the ASIS Workshop of Computer Composition.* Washington, DC: American Society for Information Science, 1971.

Lee, Marshall, *Bookmaking: The Illustrated Guide to Design and Production.* R. R. Bowker Company, 1965.

Lehmann-Haupt, Hellmut; Wroth, Lawrence C.; and Silver, Rollo G., *The Book in America: A History of the*

Making and Selling of Books in the United States. 2d ed. R. R. Bowker Company, 1951.

Mayer, Martin, *About Television.* Harper & Row, Publishers, Inc., 1972.

McCuen, Jo Ray, and Winkler, Anthony C., *Readings for Writers.* Harcourt Brace Jovanovich, Inc., 1974.

Mitchell, John H., *Writing for Professional and Technical Journals.* John Wiley & Sons, Inc., 1968.

Mok, Michael, "The Radcliffe Experiment," *Publishers Weekly,* Aug. 7, 1972.

National Association of Broadcasters, *Careers in Radio.*

———, *Careers in Television.* Booklets, available from NAB, 1771 N Street, NW, Washington, DC 20036.

Nicholson, Margaret, *A Dictionary of American-English Usage.* Oxford University Press, 1957.

———, *A Practical Style Guide for Authors and Editors.* Holt, Rinehart, & Winston, Inc., 1967.

Petersen, Clarence, *The Bantam Story: Thirty Years of Paperback Publishing.* Rev. ed. Bantam Books, Inc., 1975.

Redding, W. Charles, and Sanborn, George A., *Business and Industrial Communication.* Harper & Row, Publishers, Inc., 1964.

Ross, Billy I., and Hileman, Donald G., *Where Shall I Go to Study Advertising?* Lubbock, TX: Texas Tech University, n.d. Booklet, available from Dr. Billy I. Ross, Department of Marketing, Texas Tech University, Lubbock, TX 79409.

Sandage, Charles H., and Fryburger, Vernon, *Advertising: Theory and Practice.* 8th ed. Richard D. Irwin, Inc., 1971.

Sanderson, Arthur M., *Iowa Newspaper Desk Book and Guide to Good Writing.* Iowa City, IA: The University of Iowa Extension Division, n.d.

Sherman, Theodore A., and Johnson, Simon S., *Modern Technical Writing,* 3d ed. Prentice-Hall, Inc., 1975.

Small, William, *To Kill a Messenger: Television News and the Real World.* Hastings House, Publishers, Inc., 1970.

Smith, Roger H., *Paperback Parnassus.* Westview Press, 1976.

Tichy, Henrietta J., *Effective Writing for Engineers—Managers—Scientists.* John Wiley & Sons, Inc., 1966.

Terrell, Neil, *Power Technique for Radio-TV Copywriting.* Tab Books, 1971.

Trapnell, Coles, *Teleplay: An Introduction to Television Writing.* Rev. ed. Hawthorn Books, Inc., 1974.

U.S. Department of Labor, *Employment Outlook for Advertising, Marketing Research, and Public Relations Workers.* Washington, DC: Government Printing Office, n.d. Booklet, available from Superintendent of Documents, Government Printing Office, Washington, DC 20402.

Unwin, Stanley, *The Truth About a Publisher.* The Macmillan Company, 1960.

Warburg, Frederic, *An Occupation for Gentlemen.* Houghton Mifflin Company, 1960.

Weyr, Thomas, "Getting Into Publishing," *Publishers Weekly,* March 24, 1975.

Wilson, Adrian, *The Design of Books.* Peregrine Smith, Inc., 1974. Reprint of earlier edition.

Zinsser, William, *On Writing Well: An Informal Guide to Writing Nonfiction.* Harper & Row, Publishers, Inc., 1976.

Index

Accounting, 73, 102–103
Actor, 71, 76, 77, 117
Adams, Franklin P., 25
Advertising, 10, 36–48 (Ch. 4), 65, 72, 76, 101
  agencies, 38
  courses, list of, 44
  field of, 36–37
  how advertising works, 37–43
  job, getting a, 45–46
  job satisfactions, 36–37, 48
  in magazines, 32
  media, list of, 38
  qualifications for career, 37, 44–45
  salaries, 36, 48
  service and supply houses, list of, 38
Advertising: job classifications
  account executive, 40–41
  advertising manager, 39–40
  agency head, 40
  art director, 41
  artist, 41
  broadcast time sales representative, 43
  copy chief, 41
  copywriter, 41, 46–48
  direct mail specialist, 43
  director of radio or television, 42
  layout person, 41
  media director, 42
  new-business person, 41
  production assistant, 42
  production manager, 42
  promotion manager, 43
  publicity director, 42
  research assistant, 42
  research director, 42
  space buyer, 42
  space sales representative, 43
American Council on Education for Journalism, 124
Art and design, 19–20, 32, 33, 41, 76, 87, 92–94
Asimov, Isaac, 61
Association of American Publishers, 108
Authors, 86–95

Bernstein, Carl, 13
Bernstein, Theodore, *The Careful Writer,* 58
Bly, Nellie, 13
Book publishing, 79–110 (Ch. 7)
  book business, 79–80
  departments in a publishing house, 82–103
  courses in, 130–141
  how book publishing works, 81–82
  job, getting a, 105–109
  job satisfactions, 110
  qualifications for career, 104–105
  salaries, 109
  style of a publishing house, 82
  textbooks versus trade books, 81, 96
  women in, 105
Book publishing: accounting, 102–103
Book publishing: authors
  advances and royalties for, 87–88
  and designers, 93–94
  and editors and publishers, 84–90
  typescript preparation and proofreading by, 89, 90, 92
Book publishing: design and designers, 87, 92–94
  and authors and editors, 93–94
  of children's books, 96
  duties of, 92

  free-lance, 96, 109–110
  future of, 94
  paperbacks, 96
  and photocomposition, 93
  and production, 92–93
Book publishing: editing and editors, 81, 83–88
  and authors, 85–87
  copy-editor, 88–90
  editorial committee, 87
  editor in chief, 84–85
  first reader, 83
  literary agents, 85, 87–88
  proofreading, 90–92; and computer composition, 91
  specialists, 85
  typescripts: importance of, 84–85; unsolicited, 83, 85
Book publishing: management, 103
Book publishing: marketing, 81, 97–102
  book clubs, 99
  book reviews, 101–102
  bookstores, 98–99
  direct marketing, 99
  foreign markets, 101
  libraries, 100
  marketing manager, 97
  mass market, 83, 99, 107
  paperbacks, 87, 99
  sales representatives, 98–99
  subsidiary rights, 99–100
  technical books, 101
  textbooks, 100–101
  trade books, 101

Book publishing: production, 87, 94–97
bookbinding, 95, 97
computer composition, 91–92, 97
facsimile editions, 97
photocomposition versus hot type, 93
printing and printers, 93, 95, 97
procuring services and supplies, 95–96
production manager, 95–96
schedule for producing a book, 96
size of staff, 96
Brinkley, David, 24
Broadcasting: radio and television, 70–78 (Ch. 6)
early broadcasts: radio, 70; television, 71
electronic media, 70–72
how a broadcasting station works, 72–77
job, getting a, 24–25, 78
job satisfactions, 78
networks, 70–71; network shows, 71–73
radio's "fragmented" audience, 71
scripts, movie and television, 11–12, 83
source of programs, 73
Broadcasting: job classifications
actor, 71, 76, 77
chief engineer, 76
continuity writer, 76
controller, 73

farm director, 75
film director, 75
general manager, 72–73
graphic artist, 76
local program director, 73–74
musician, 71, 77
network jobs, 77
news camerapeople, 75
newscaster, 75
news director, 75
newswriter, 75
producer-director, 74
production manager, 74
promotion manager, 76
reporter, 75
sales manager, 76–77
special program performer, 74–75
sportscaster, 75
staff announcer, 74
technician, 76
traffic manager, 77
Broun, Heywood, 23
Buying. See Procurement

Cartoonists, 19–20
Ceram, C. W. See Marek, Kurt W.
Chancellor, John, 24
Chavis, Jane, 108
Colorado State University, 34
Communications industry, 10–11
Communications, schools of, 10–11
Consumers, 36, 37
Copy-editing, 88–90
Copyreading, 23–24

149

Copywriting, 41, 46–48
Crichton, Michael, *The Andromeda Strain*, 60
Cronkite, Walter, 24
Cryptograms, 55–56

Davis, Richard Harding, 13
Design. *See* Art and design
Direct mail, 43, 99
Doubleday & Company, Inc., 104, 105–106

Eckerd College, 123
Economics, writing on, 19
Editing and editors, 32–34, 50–53, 66–68, 81, 83–88, 90
Editor and Publisher, 17
Education, 111–141 (Ch. 8)
Educational courses, 35, 44–45, 105, 130–141
Educational institutions, 10, 11, 15–16, 34, 60, 97, 123
Educational programs, 18, 97, 112–123, 124–129
  accredited programs in communications, 124–129
  for broadcasting, 129
  at Denver, University of, 120
  Harvard/Radcliffe summer course, 106, 118–120
  at Modern Media Institute, 123
  at New York University, 117–118

at Pratt Institute, 122–123
in publishing houses, 108
at Rochester Institute of Technology, 120–122
at South Florida, University of, 112–117
summer internship on newspaper, 18
Engineer, 10, 49, 65–66, 68–69, 76, 77

Finances, reporting on, 23
Future of
  books, 79
  design, 94
  newspapers, 27–28
  proofreading, 91

Green, Ashbel, 106–107

Harding, Warren, 27
Harper & Row, Publishers, Inc., 104, 105

Jefferson, Thomas, 13
Job classifications, 19–20, 22–27, 32, 39–43, 63–69, 72–77, 82–103
Jobs, 12, 14–15, 17–20, 24–27, 35, 45–46, 60–61, 77–78, 103, 105–109
Job satisfactions, 25, 28–29, 36–37, 69, 78, 110

Kennedy, John F., 27
Kiplinger Report, 26
Knopf, Alfred A., Inc., 104, 105, 106, 108

Libraries, 66, 100
Literary agents, 12, 85, 87–88

Magazines, 30–35 (Ch. 3)
  how a magazine works, 31–34
  job, getting a, 35
  magazine business, 30–31
  photocomposition of, 33
  qualifications for career, 34–35
  types of, 31
Magazines: circulation department, 32
Magazines: editorial department, 32–34
  associate or assistant editor, 32
  chief editor, 32
  copy editor, 32
  editorial assistant, 32
  managing editor, 32
  researcher, 32–33
Magazines: graphics department, 32, 33
Magazines: promotion department, 32
Magazines: sales department—advertising space, 32
Management, 40, 72–73, 103–104
Marek, Kurt W., *Götter, Gräber, und Gelehrter (Gods, Graves and Scholars)*, 60–61
Marketing, 32, 43, 65, 76–77, 87, 97–102

Mason/Charter Publishers, Inc., 105, 107
Missouri, University of, 34
Musician, 71, 77

National Geographic, 34, 58, 79
News media, 10–11, 13–29 (Ch. 2)
  building a career in, 21–24
  future of newspapers, 27–28
  job, getting a, 15, 17–20
  job satisfactions, 25, 28–29
  news business, 13–14
  news services, 22
  qualifications for employees, 15–17
  salaries, 14–15
  small versus large newspapers, 18–19
  suburban newspapers, 19
  summer internship, 18
News media: alternatives to newspaper jobs, 24–27
  politician or assistant to politician, 26–27
  newscaster, 24–25
  newsmagazines and newsletters, writer for, 25–26
  public relations, personnel in, 26
News media: job classifications
  cartoonist, 19–20
  columnist, 20

151

consumer affairs reporter, 23
copyreader, 23–24
crime reporter, 23
drama critic, 19
financial or economics specialist, 19, 23
foreign correspondent, 20, 23
health news reporter, 23
literary critic, 19
music critic, 19
newswriter, 10, 21, 50
science newswriter, 10, 19
social news reporter, 23
sportswriter, 10, 22–23
Newsweek, 25, 32
New Yorker, The, 58, 60
New York Times, The, 22, 23
Northwestern University, 34

O'Connor, Patrick, 107

Patents, 49, 61, 64–65
Pegler, Westbrook, 23
Perkins, Maxwell, 81, 86
Philadelphia *Bulletin,* 7, 21
Playboy, 79
Politics, 26–27
Popular Library, Inc., 104, 105, 107, 108
Printing and printers, 52–54, 93, 95, 97
Procurement, 41–42, 95–96
Production, 42, 74, 94–97
Promotion, 32, 43, 65, 76
Proofreading, 90–92

Publicity, 42
Publishers, 85, 104–109
Pyle, Ernie, 13

Qualifications of personnel, 15–17, 34–35, 37, 44–45, 54–59, 104–105

Random House, Inc., 108
Rensselaer Polytechnic Institute, 60
Research, 32–33, 42–43
Reston, James, 22
Rice, Grantland, 23
Richardson, Stewart, 105–106

Salaries, 14–15, 19, 36, 48, 68–69, 109
Sales. *See* Marketing
Sales representative, 32, 43, 76, 98–99
Saturday Review, 58
Saunders, W. B., Company, 85
Science and scientists, 10, 19, 65–66
Scientific American, 54, 58
Scripts, movie and television, 11–12
Sevareid, Eric, 24
Smith, Red, 23
Spivak, Alvin, 21–22
Sports, 22–23, 71, 75
Standard Advertising Register, 45–46
Stevenson, Adlai E., 27
Syracuse University, 34

Technical writer: alternative jobs
  advertising, 65
  editing, 66–68
  library work, 66
  patent agent, 64–65
  promotion, 65
  sales, 65
  science or engineering, 65–66
Technical writer: qualifications, 54–59
  logical mind, 54–56
  sensitivity to language, 56–59
Technical writing, 10, 49–69 (Ch. 5)
  copy—creation, computer processing, printing, 51–54
  definition of, 50–51
  editing of, 66–68; freelance, 67
  field of, 49–51
  handling a specific assignment, 63
  how technical writing works, 51–54
  job, getting a, 60–61
  job satisfactions, 69
  salaries, 68–69
Technical writing: types of
  house organs, 49
  patent disclosures, 49
  progress reports, 49, 59
  specification writing, 63–64
  technical papers and speeches, 49
Time, 25, 30, 32
Tonero, Jane, 107
Traffic management, 77, 95
Type composition
  computer, 51–54, 91, 97
  hot type, 53–54, 93
  photocomposition, 33, 93
Typescripts, 11, 83–85

United Press International, 22
U.S. News & World Report, 25
University presses, 109

Venn, Mrs. Diggory, 119

Wall Street Journal, The, 97
White, E. B., 57
Wilson, Edmund, 60
Wolfe, Thomas, 86
Woodward, Robert, 13
Writers
  free-lance, 9–11, 31–32
  staff, 9–10, 31–32
  See also Authors
Wyeth, M. S., Jr., 106

Zenger, John Peter, 13